CRACKING
THE
BUSINESS
DEVELOPMENT
CODE

$$BD = M + S + CS$$

7 SMALL STEPS FOR YOU
1 GIANT LEAP FOR YOUR BUSINESS

C. STEVEN JONES

innovo
PUBLISHING

Published by Innovo Publishing, LLC
www.innovopublishing.com
1-888-546-2111

Providing Full-Service Publishing Services for Christian Authors,
Artists & Ministries:
Books, eBooks, Audiobooks, Music, Film & Courses

CRACKING THE BUSINESS DEVELOPMENT CODE
7 Small Steps for You, 1 Giant Leap for Your Business

ISBN: 978-1-61314-519-7

Cover Design & Interior Layout: Innovo Publishing, LLC

Printed in the United States of America
U.S. Printing History
First Edition: 2019

ENDORSEMENTS

"This book takes the complex and misunderstood subject of business development and frames it into a clearly defined concept that is a must read for any B2B business leader. The 7 step evaluation process is a compelling, accurate, and thought-provoking exercise that, without a doubt, will ensure explosive growth within any organization."

—J. Darrell Lynn, Serial Entrepreneur: President and CEO, Blink Home, Vintique, and multiple online home furnishing companies

"Steve brings a refreshing and unique take on business development. His 'three pillars' are very relatable and actionable for any company in B2B sales. Read this book, put it into practice, and watch your business development team turn into a business development engine that works!"

—Marisa Pensa, President & Co-Founder, Competitive Selling (a sales training company)

"Steve has provided an outstanding look into the subject of business development. In this book he has taken a challenging and complex subject and presented it in a simple and easy to understand way. The thoughts and concepts in this book will bring insight to those that are aspiring to become successful in business development while at the same time challenge those that are already seasoned and experienced. Steve's ideas come from years of personal experience and success, and I have little doubt that it will lead its readers to that same success."

—Jeff L. Arnold, President & CEO,
Fisher and Arnold, Inc.

"My friend Steve Jones has combined his many years of actual experience, observation, and thought about business development and given us an extremely useful and practical guide. If you touch any aspect of your company's business development process, this book will both encourage you and make you better at your job. I'll recommend it to all my clients."

—Ken Edmundson, CEO, The Edmundson Group;
Author; Founder of the ShortTrack Business
Management System

CONTENTS

INTRODUCTION

Welcome to *Cracking the Business Development Code*. During the relatively short time we as human beings are granted on this Earth, the most precious commodity God has given to us is time. Time is the currency of life, and I am most grateful that you have chosen to invest some of yours reading this book. I hope you find it worthwhile.

About a year ago, I was at a trade show and technical conference in Atlanta when a very well-dressed, professional young man walked up to me and handed me his business card. What's the first thing we always do when someone hands us a card? We look at their title, of course. His read, "Business Development Director." *Wow*, I thought, *he seemed very young to be given such a key leadership role.* I was impressed.

After several minutes of delightful and engaging technical conversation, it became obvious that he was selling pumps for one of the major manufacturers in a specific geographic area. He was a regional pump sales guy. Pretty straightforward. He was no doubt filling a very noble and critical role in his organization (we will talk about that later), but still, it was quite simple. Sales rep. I remember thinking to myself, *How did a sales rep morph into a business development director? What exactly did he direct?*

This encounter caused me to reflect on my own journey of thirty years in the sales and marketing space, the roles I have had, and just how things have evolved. Most of my career has been spent in what we refer to as B2B—business to business: businesses providing products and services to other businesses. Not to be confused with B2C (business to consumer) or B2G (business to government) and the host of others that I shall not list here (I just love all the nifty acronyms we create). Although I have spent quite a bit of time and energy in both the B2C and B2G spaces, it is important to point out that the focus of this work will be directed more towards the B2B marketplace than any other. More specifically to the small- to medium-sized companies that dominate the business landscape in the U.S. today. These concepts apply to anyone in any market engaged in what they refer to as *business development*, but my experience and therefore the real value of this book will be in the world of small- to medium-sized businesses, selling goods and services to other businesses.

I continued to ponder this extremely versatile two-word phrase: "business development." What a powerful, overused, and misunderstand idiom. Is it a verb? A noun? An adjective? Or all the above? What exactly does it mean?

The revelation I had that day in Atlanta and my personal observations since is that the development of business and the way we go about it appears to have evolved over the last twenty or so years—and not necessarily for the good. Have you ever taken a simple idea and complicated the crud out of it? I know I have. My wife tells me that I analyze and complicate things to death all the time. And of course, she is right. As of late, there has been a lot written and said about the process of *continuous improvement*. I firmly believe that this is a valuable thing, and that through the principles of continuous improvement, the methods and processes we use in business development will keep becoming more and more effective. The products we create will become better and more useful to us all. Technology would not be expanding at such an exponential rate if it were not for continuous improvement and innovation. This process makes our standard of living better and our systems much more efficient.

However, I have also heard it said that Thomas Edison did not invent the lightbulb through continuous improvement of the candle. I believe this is especially true in the case of business development. For some reason, we have steered away from simple and basic principles and segregated our organizations into these complex silos that sometimes seem to be competing with themselves. We automate and convolute to a point of incompetency. It almost feels like the more complicated and confusing we make it, the better we think it will be. Our sales and marketing teams have come to rely so heavily on technology and computers, digital marketing science, and the psychological manipulation of the buyer that we have forgotten that developing business is really about people.

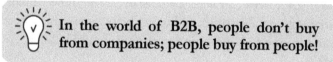

In the world of B2B, people don't buy from companies; people buy from people!

The fundamental ideas of this book will attempt to bring our thoughts about business development back on track and remind ourselves of the common-sense ideas that have not changed much in a thousand years. Principles that were used in the market squares of ancient Rome are as vividly applicable today as they were then. Those B2B firms and companies that understand and embrace this already have a distinct advantage and will continue to thrive, capture market share, and sustain long-term growth.

Over the past three decades, I have watched, read, listened to, participated in, managed, and absorbed an extensive variety of corporate marketing ideas, sales, and business growth initiatives, consumer-based sales training programs, go-to market plans, elaborate e-marketing campaigns, and fresh and new innovative sales ideas. There have been literally millions of books, tapes, seminar packages, and videos written and created that cover an infinite spectrum of business development techniques. It is both staggering and overwhelming. Many of these have substantial merit and bring real value to the reader, while many others do not.

It also seems that everyone is a business development expert these days and is desperately trying to seek a new and better "mousetrap." Many are simply opinions with no real basis in fact or a restatement of someone else's view repackaged in a different format. Please don't get me wrong, there are a lot of smart people promoting sound ideas and proven sales techniques today. I have read and listened to a lot of folks that make good sense. In no way am I trying to minimize those credible authors. My goal here is not to demean the stimulation of creative thinking and the search for a better process or to share some new whizbang marketing or sales process but to help frame up how the overall business development machine should look, act, and work.

Although I do read as many new books and articles as I can, I find myself relying more on the timeless works written by true visionary leaders like Tom Peters, Dave Ramsey, John Maxwell, Zig Ziegler, and Peter Drucker, that provide guidance and essential baselines for any business development program. They all have a common theme of basic and fundamental methods—fundamentals that typically combine proven statistics, science, innovation, and sound common sense and that revolve around servant leadership, biblical principles, trust, integrity, and customer centric ideals. Timeless mentoring that will always apply to good and sound business development planning, regardless of the product or venue.

This is also not about some revolutionary new marketing or sales gimmick or process. The basis of the following concept is about a philosophy of synergy and realignment of what you should already have in place in your organization. What I will attempt to bring together for you in the following pages is what I have come to believe are the pillars of business development and how to approach them for the common good of the customer and the organization. I have divided the material into two distinct parts:

1. The Philosophy
2. The Steps

The first section outlines the three essential elements surrounding the philosophy of the trilogy concept of business development, what I have learned, and why it is important. The second section provides for a seven-step evaluation process to follow as a guide to ensure your company or group is structured for success. After all, being able to say that we provide maximum service and value to any client we touch should be our company mission.

Peter Drucker was an American management consultant and author who contributed greatly to the foundation of modern business and has been described as "the father of modern management."[1] In his book *The Practice of Management*, he shared with us that the primary purpose of any business is to make a customer.[2] OK, that sounds simple. But I contend that this idea should also be expanded to include, "to retain a customer." Marketing research has suggested that it is five to seven times more difficult to gain a new customer than to retain existing ones—to not have a *consumer* but a *customer* for the duration. Someone to be *courted*, *dated*, and subsequently *married* for a loyal and long-term relationship that benefits both parties. The result is something called *client loyalty*. We will talk much more about that later as well.

At this point, it is very important to point out that this singleness of purpose, this focus on making and retaining loyal, committed, and repeat clients is the *real core focus* of this

---

1. Described as such by *Businessweek Magazine* and the Drucker Institute. "Peter F. Drucker, Father of Modern Management, Dies at 95," *The Seattle Times,* November 2005. www.seattletimes.com/business/peter-f-drucker-father-of-modern-management-dies-at-95/.

2. Peter Drucker, *The Practice of Management* (NY: Harper Collins, 1954).

book. That should be the holy grail, the main takeaway, the crowning achievement of any business development initiative.

With that in mind, here are four simple truths of business development (see *Figure 1*):

The Four Truths of Business Development

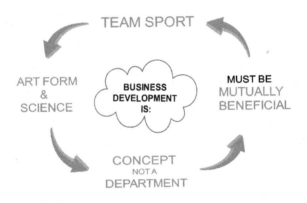

Figure 1: The Four Truths of Business Development

1. Business development is a team sport.

2. Business development is both an art form and a science.

3. Business development is a concept, not a department!

4. Business development is an endeavor that must be mutually beneficial.

It is not merely the number of sales calls or pre-established quotas or website hits or click throughs or successful advertising campaigns or average wait time for customer calls or wins vs. new hots identified as separate initiatives—but all those things together. Business development is a comprehensive, overarching philosophy that encompasses all these things as well as three clear and closely connected elements that, in my opinion, form the foundation for any successful business development *engine*. Throughout this text, we will refer to our *business development engine* frequently. That's because, like an internal combustion engine, there are three major components that are absolutely required for it to come to life and provide power. Air, fuel, and spark. Once those are in harmony, then power is produced, and it becomes the life force for whatever endeavor it is assigned. Business development is that life force, and providing power for businesses and customers is the fuel. A well-tuned and balanced business development engine is the keystone to the health and growth of any company.

As we dive into the logic and information in the pages that follow, all I ask is that you be open minded and willing to consider a different view of the way we think about and deploy the concept of business development.

OK then . . . let's get started.

PART 1:

THE
TRILOGY
PHILOSOPHY
OF
BUSINESS
DEVELOPMENT

Truly successful growth companies do not chase the sale or the project; they chase relationships.

WHAT IS BUSINESS DEVELOPMENT, REALLY?

I n the early 1990s, I migrated from a technical project manager to my first soirée into the world of sales and business development. I went to work for a Fortune 100 firm that was involved in selling industrial process systems and equipment and the associated design, engineering, and project management services that surrounded these rather large industrial facilities—paper mills, power plants, boilers, recycling facilities, etc. Unlike my associates in the company that sold individual pieces of hardware or replacement parts, our mission was to foster relationships with owners, developers, constructors, architects, and design firms that would take a project from a design or concept and turn it into a reality.

There were many moving parts to these business journeys, including project proformas and finance, conceptual design and detailed engineering, procurement of materials and equipment, project scheduling and management, as well as commissioning and startup. Some of these endeavors could take months and sometimes years to complete. The overall sales effort would always engage many departments within our company and demand the commitment, teamwork, and input from each one. We called this complex team effort the development of business: business development. Today these types of firms are referred to as EPC (engineer/procure/construct) and are heavily engaged in this same type of approach.

But we understood even then that a business developer was a very different role than a salesperson or an account representative and required a different mindset and approach. Even though at the time, I had no appreciation for how important the cross interaction of all the departments truly was to the success of these project wins and the overall health of the company, we did understand clearly that business development was a verb and absolutely a team sport.

Now we fast forward twenty years. Things have changed quite a lot and the sales landscape is very different. The term *business development manager* has appeared magically on the scene, and it seems to be used as a synonym to generally describe any type of salesperson or account representative or telemarketer. I suppose since the word *sales* has taken on such a negative connotation, we needed a smoother, more elegant-sounding moniker, and *business development manager* sort of just rolls off your tongue. It certainly sounds better. Either salespeople have the need to feel more important and empowered or their bosses want potential clients to think their person is a little stronger or faster than the competitor.

Truth be known, I too am guilty of following the trend and using this title myself. I have held this title personally and hired sales staff and put that on their business cards. After all, do not sales folks develop business for their firm? Sure, they do. Anyone that has been a salesperson knows that we manage a variety of things like schedules, events, meetings, product deliveries, and our own time.

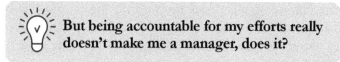

But being accountable for my efforts really doesn't make me a manager, does it?

It's misleading and somewhat confusing for both clients and employees.

Regardless, we still ask, What is business development? As my grandfather would always say, "Son, that is the sixty-four-dollar question."[3] If you ask ten sales managers, VPs of business development, or even CEOs of companies to define business development, you will get a wide variety of different but similar answers. This phrase has come to mean a host of varying things, and as mentioned earlier, has evolved quite a lot over the past twenty years. However, to better understand the true meaning of business development, let's start by dissecting this phrase and breaking it into its two basic parts.

We shall begin by defining the word *business*. According to Merriam-Webster.com, as it applies to our context, the definition is,

 Business:

The activity of making, buying, or selling goods or providing services in exchange for money coming from the Middle English word bisynesse, meaning bisy (busy) + nesse (ness) with the first known use in 14th century.[4]

That is pretty straightforward: providing goods and services for money. *Busyness*. Hmm . . . I have heard it said many

---

3. "One of the most popular radio quiz shows during the 1940s was Take It or Leave It in which contestants strived to answer question after question until they reached the top prize of sixty-four silver dollars." Farlex Dictionary of Idioms. S.v. *$64 question*. Retrieved June 11, 2019, from https://idioms.thefreedictionary.com/%2464+question.

4. Merriam-Webster.com, keyword: *business*. This is a compilation of phrases used under this term on the website.

times that being busy does not mean being productive. But I digress.

Now let's get another opinion from Dictionary.com, as it relates in noun form to our context:

 Business:

The purchase and sale of goods in an attempt to make a profit.[5]

Again, a very similar theme. So we have determined that the definition of *business* is the activity of exchanging goods and services for money with the objective of making a profit. Simple enough. The word *profit* can mean a variety of things, and it is important here to note that many terrific businesses and organizations are chartered as "non-profit" and operate under a different set of tax regulations than "for-profit" companies. But for purposes of our discussion, we will assume an equal playing field with all having the same basic objective. Whether profit to you means money, equity, time, surplus goods for the food bank, or raising donations to build a new school in Haiti, the goal for any business development team is the same.

Now let us move to the next magic word in our phrase: *development.* Going back to Merriam-Webster, we shall define the word *development* as it relates to our concept:

 Development:

The act or process of growing or causing something to grow or become larger or more advanced; the act or process of creating something over a period of time; the state of being created or made more advanced.[6]

---

5. Dictionary.com, keyword: *business.*
6. Merriam-Webster.com, keyword: *development.*

According to the Cambridge Dictionary, the definition of *development* is,

 Development:

Growth or changes that make something become more advanced.[7]

To combine these two similar definitions for the word *development*, it would be safe to say that development is the act of creating, changing, or growing something over time to a more advanced state.

Now let's consider some other parallel concepts where development is a key factor. In the game of chess, the development of a piece means to bring that piece into play from its initial position on a player's back rank. In photography, when a print is immersed in the right chemicals, it is brought into sharp focus and referred to as being "developed." Therefore, any way you choose to spin it, development is a universal idea.

Armed with these definitions, I have combined them all into a single statement to help us merge the two words (*business development*) into a single concept:

 Business development is the process of creating, enhancing, or growing the activity of exchanging goods and services for money with the objective to make a profit, over time, to a more advanced and mutually beneficial state.

Take a minute and let that really sink in . . . and focus on the word *process*. It's not an act, but a process.

---

7. Dictionary.Cambridge.org, keyword: *development.*

Business development is also the creation of long-term value for an organization, from earning loyal customers, markets, and relationships. There is elegance in this simplicity. Consider this abstract thought:

> Business development is about seeking out the best ground, applying the right fertilizer and chemicals, diligently placing seeds, tending the garden, and growing your own food in order to feed your company family.

OK, you say, *help me understand all this.* It is really very simple. Business development is not sales. Business development is not marketing. Business development is not a noun name for a specific person, job, activity, or department within your company. Business development is not the act of looking for new clients or responding to a request for a proposal. Business development is not being just an account representative or a graphic designer, or a webmaster or a customer service agent. *It is being all these things in a symphony of concerted effort.*

> Business development is the art of making a company more valuable to clients and more competitive in existing and new markets.

It incorporates enhancing the company's image or brand while working with other departments to increase the overall product or service value to clients.

Another key responsibility of the business development engine is to create as much enthusiasm for the product/service/company internally as externally. We have been value programmed to believe that business development is synonymous with sales as a stand-alone effort, but it is not. Once you grasp the idea that business development is a concept with many factors of influence and one focus then you are ready to consider the details that follow.

GROWTH MUST BE INTENTIONAL

Before we move any further, consider the statement that "growth must be intentional." The premise of this text and the thoughts contained herein are focused on the growth of a company through its business development effort and ideals. There are some companies, however, that do not want to grow. And that is perfectly OK.

I have a friend and colleague who owns and operates a professional services firm. His wife is the president and he is the vice president. They have about eight staff members and do exceptional work in their market in a localized geography. They are like a little family. They have a small list of very dedicated clients and are quite happy with their volume of projects and revenue annually. When I have tried to "help" them with advice on how to grow the business, they tell me they don't want my advice. I have a deep respect for people who know what they want. They have reached cruising altitude and are *intentionally maintaining to keep pace with inflation.*

Conversely, there are some companies that simply don't think about intentional growth. My stepfather (whom I loved and respected immensely) and his business partner started and operated a successful manufacturing company from about 1980 until 2015 when they sold the business. They employed about two hundred and fifty people and made an essential but non-glamorous product. His partner was the business and sales guy, and my stepfather was the operational brains. They had a great partnership.

During their thirty-five years in business together, all the "sales" was performed by one person, my stepfather's partner. They never had a website, no marketing team or public relations firm, and no salespeople (they did use dealer reps). Brochures were mostly product data sheets, and customer service was handled by the office manager. Their growth was unintentional and through *osmosis*. They still managed to eventually create a fairly substantial business, but what could it have been if they had been intentional about business growth?

Some years ago, in one of many strategy sessions that I have been involved with, I remember hearing a member of senior leadership say, "I don't mind aggressive growth as long as there is no risk." There is no such thing. Substantial growth requires some level of risk. The pages that follow are about how to position, structure, and execute for substantial growth. If you are happy with where you are and what you are doing, then by all means, stay put and enjoy life. Nothing wrong at all with that. If, on the other hand, you have never given it much thought, or you have tried and not had the success you desire, then I firmly believe you will find the concepts, ideas, and information shared in the following pages to be extremely useful.

SINGLENESS OF PURPOSE: CLIENT LOYALTY

 Business development is a concept, and it has one primary goal: to create client loyalty with new and existing clients due to the overall experience the client receives from your company.

This should be the singleness of purpose for any B2B business development team. From this single vision comes growth, brand expansion, market development, profit, and all the things you desire for your company.

Learning and reading are passions for me. I try to read as much as I can these days about what others are thinking, doing, and preaching about sales, marketing, and business development. One of the most thought-provoking reads I've had in quite some time was a book by Simon Sinek called *Start with Why: How Great Leaders Inspire Everyone to Take Action*. His work had a lot of great stuff, but the fundamental takeaway for me was that successful companies are the ones that achieve client loyalty. This happens when people do not try and shop around or compare prices; they are simply willing to take your product or service, even if it is at a premium price, to do business with you and your company.

Sinek also points out that these successful companies ask themselves two basic questions: Why are we in business? Why do we do what we do?

 The implication is that passion and a desire to solve a problem in lieu of just making a profit is the key to wildly successful companies.

I agree.

The most moving and impactful message on client loyalty I have ever heard was in 2016 in Cincinnati. I was fortunate enough to attend a trade show and conference where the keynote speaker was the former director of communications strategy for Harley-Davidson Motorcycles, Ken Schmidt. I was mesmerized to say the least.

He told us that in 1985, as a specialist in corporate positioning and media relations, he was asked to work with the struggling Harley-Davidson Motorcycle company to help change the company's image and create demand. In 1969, American Machine and Foundry (AMF) had bought Harley and lowered the standards of manufacturing, which subsequently created lower-quality, poorly built motorcycles. They leaked oil, broke down a lot, and were given nicknames like "Hardly Ableson," "Hardly Driveable," and "Hogly Ferguson"—which, by the way, is where the nickname "Hog" originated. In addition, the 1960s and early 1970s saw the rise of the outlaw motorcycle gangs, which seemed to make Harley the ride of choice. When anyone heard the name "Harley Davidson," the image of a greasy criminal biker wearing nasty jeans, a red bandana, and black engineer's boots came to mind.

In his talk, Schmidt shared strategy, stories, and insights on how the team went about changing that image. They changed the business model and vastly improved the manufactured quality of the product. They also decided on a different marketing vision to change the image and culture of the company to reflect a different target client. He talked about how they demanded that all dealers change the way they addressed new customers when they came into a Harley dealership. No longer would they say, "How may I help you?" but they would say, rather, "Welcome to the Harley family! We are glad you are here." His team created what is known as the Harley lifestyle. Owning a Harley was not about transportation but about a "way of life." They succeeded in creating a fanatically loyal customer base and a passionately loyal culture. He said they created disciples.

As a direct result of a very intentional effort, Harley-Davidson became one of the most visible and frequently reported-on companies in the world, while sales of its motorcycles rocketed.

That is what I mean by creating client loyalty.

THE TRILOGY
CONCEPT

L et me say this again, in case you didn't hear me clearly in the last chapter, because it's of crucial importance to the central theme of this philosophical approach.

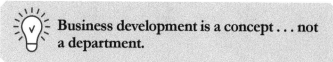

Business development is a concept . . . not a department.

The concept of business development is the responsibility of more than a single group or person or department within any company. It is the philosophy of growth, the mission of all customer-facing employees as well as all supporting members, that must be permeated throughout the ranks as a combined, intentional, and coordinated effort.

Business development is an overarching, all-inclusive initiative made up of three basic and naturally interdependent parts. Each of the parts rely heavily on the others to achieve the objective of making and sustaining clients and cannot succeed unless each part is in sync. Many companies have some level of success segmenting the parts as individually managed silos, but for any company to really reach its maximum stride, the three parts *must* be in unison.

Like any powerful, three-pronged structure, your business development engine consists of three interconnected pillars (see *Figure 2*):

The Three Pillars of Business Development

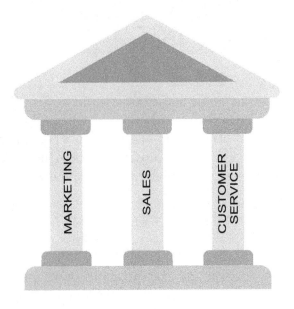

Figure 2: The Three Pillars of Business Development

1. Marketing
2. Sales
3. Customer Service

Think of a stool having three equal and required legs, each as important as the other. Your stool can be made of wood or plastic or steel or from any material you can imagine.

Some preach that customer service should be a part of the product group so that direct customer feedback can be funneled into product development. This idea has a foundation in truth and has strong merit. Listening to the client and adjusting course to provide what they want is paramount to success. However, customer service is a part of business development.

 Great care should be taken to ensure that customer feedback is funneled unfiltered to product development but not at the risk of segregating customer service from the trilogy.

Many companies today have even chosen to have marketing and sales in-house, while outsourcing customer service as a third-party call center function with firms in a variety of countries around the world. That is baffling. If the lion's share of revenue and 100 percent of repeat business comes from the efforts of the customer service pillar of the engine, why on earth would a company farm it out to some third-party firm in a third world country that has no vested interest in the success of the team?

This may not seem like a revelation just yet, but as I asked earlier, please keep an open mind. If you allow yourself to let go of the paradigms we have had ingrained for years about sales, marketing, customer service, and all the different combinations of silos, departments, and structures businesses use, it will slowly begin to make perfect sense.

THE POWER OF THREE

Before we move on, take a moment and consider the trilogy of marketing, sales, and customer service and the absolute *power of three.* Have you ever noticed that the universe seems to be made up of threes? Consider these examples:

1. The color that you see on any TV screen was derived from what is called RGB (red, green, and blue colors). From these three primary colors, almost any color can be depicted.

2. The rule of three or power of three is a writing principle that suggests that things that come in threes are funnier, more satisfying, or more effective than other numbers of things. The rule of three is also based on the technique that people tend to remember three things. In speeches and presentations, we see that it comes up time and time again. Three has power.[9]

3. Why is a stool more stable than, say, a table with four legs? The geometric reason lies in the fact that it only takes three points to define a plane. Any point that is added to that plane will make it harder and harder for the plane to be stable.

4. We have already mentioned the example of the three life-giving elements of an internal combustion engine: air, fuel, and spark.

5. Clint Eastwood had a lot of luck with *The Good, The Bad and The Ugly.*

6. P. T. Barnum found three rings was the optimum, visually, for people's attention span at the circus.

7. The triangle is the strongest of geometric shapes.

8. In the immortal words of King Solomon, "A cord of three strands is not easily broken" (Ecclesiastes 4:9–12).

9. Then, of course, there is the ultimate power of three: The Father, the Son, and the Holy Spirit.

---

9. This premise is based on my research, experience, and knowledge of the topic.

The point is that it is no accident that three is a recurring theme in nature. On that day in Atlanta when I realized that business development had moved away from what it should be, that moment of clarity also gave me vision as to what business development really consisted of—and it was also subject to the power of three.

As shown in *Figure 3*, using the stool analogy, business development is a concept that exemplifies the power of three, and when properly structured, is an unstoppable force.

Business Development Stool

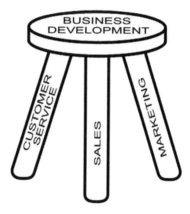

Figure 3: Business Development Stool

NEXT STEP

Now that we have had a little history lesson, learned about the power of three, established what business development *is not*, what its basic elements consist of, and broken it down into what business development really means, the next step of our journey will be a closer look at each of the three legs

33

or "pillars"—to explore at a macro level the role each plays in the trilogy.

Understand that each of these three functions are vastly complex, and tons of great material, science, and opinions exist pertaining to each. The intent herein is not to provide an in-depth drill down on each topic but to provide an overview of the basic elements, key ideas, and impact each has on the success of the whole.

With some of the pieces you may already be very well versed, with some you may not. The idea is to explain in simple terms all the moving parts and what they mean and to share the items that have proven to be the most important. For your business development engine to operate as a whole, grasping the idea that business development is a concept is a *must*. As we move ahead, you will better understand *why*. Now let's take a closer look at each of the three main parts of the whole.

3

MARKETING

B2B marketing is about knowing who your customer is and then delivering your company's message of value to that potential client's need.

The first pillar of our trilogy stool is marketing. What a powerful word: *marketing*. Gives me chill bumps just saying it. Marketing is without question a very in-depth and complex portion of the business development overall effort and can be extremely overwhelming. The science of marketing has exploded over the past few years with the advent of the internet and all the digital tools at our disposal, and there are a host of options as well as thousands of gurus claiming they have the "magic" formula to grow your business. There are certainly a lot of smart people with a ton of great and timeless wisdom on this topic, but remember, marketing is simply our message to the masses.

It is very easy to get consumed by all the chaos and feel compelled to spend enormous amounts of time, resources, and money on marketing to keep pace with the competition. There is, after all, real value in effective marketing. We all have had these thoughts and fears at some point, but from a B2B perspective, it really boils down to a rather simple statement of purpose:

 B2B marketing is about knowing who your customer is and then delivering your company's message of value to that potential client's need.

Many companies today say that marketing has become so complex, they don't know how to define the best approach. But before panic sets in, let's address some basic questions:

1. What does marketing really mean, and why should I care?

2. How should a B2B marketing plan be structured?

3. What kinds of things should a B2B company focus on in marketing?

WHAT IS MARKETING?

This is a great place to start. Gary Larson is one of the greatest satirical cartoonists of our time. Very few people have not seen at least one of his cartoons somewhere, sometime. Rarely do I see one that doesn't make me chuckle, and I have always appreciated his ability to deliver a message or moral that we can all relate to in some way.

One of the folks in my office has a calendar in the hallway by his office that contains a different cartoon rendering of his each day. One day I was walking by and noticed a cartoon that really caught my eye. It depicts a man sitting in his living room with a brick in hand. Adjacent to him is the picture window that has just been broken by the brick that was obviously thrown through the window. Fragments lay scattered about the room, and he has a serious frown. Attached to the brick was a marketing flyer with the words, "Brick thrown thru your window? Call AL's Glass Repair 555-1232."

Now that is the finest example of "direct solutions marketing" I have seen in quite some time. However, I highly recommend that your team *not* use this approach.

Thankfully, real-life B2B solutions marketing is quite a bit subtler.

 In simple terms, our mission as B2B marketers is to develop a brand strategy and associated tactical methods that are designed to clearly and effectively deliver our message of value to potential and existing clients.

It is different for every company and situation, depending on a host of variables. We will discuss some of those in detail further along in the text. But first, to better understand marketing, let's drill into a little history and how this vast industry has developed.

The term we use today, *marketing*, is believed to have stemmed from the Latin word *mercatus*, meaning a marketplace or merchant. Hence the modern word *marketing* evolved from the business of trade and activity in the market squares and merchants of old. In this time, sellers who would hang baskets from long poles or display vividly colorful rugs or arrange intricate pottery in neat configurations in front of their booth spaces to entice and attract buyers at any given market were engaged in what has come to be known as, *market-ing*.

These early marketers discovered that how they displayed their goods, what colors they chose, whether the salesperson was male or female, what time of day they displayed certain items, and how they packaged items made a huge difference in their traffic and ultimately, sales success. Depending upon *whom* they were trying to target dictated how they arranged or "marketed" their products.

There have been a great number of scholars that have studied, analyzed, and published works on the history of marketing. One of the most pivotal of these is Robert Bartels' book, *The History of Marketing Thought*, written in 1976.[10] His book helped us to both grasp and understand how marketing thought has evolved. He points out that the principles of marketing have been around for thousands of years, but it was only in the late nineteenth century that we really began to apply the term as it relates to modern consumption and brand awareness. However, even though historians tell us marketing is a recent science, I again contend that the principles of basic marketing have not changed much in several millennia. The way we structure the message in today's complex market space may be different, and the vast array of delivery options have increased exponentially, but we are still trying to achieve the exact same thing that the marketers of old were: Pick my product or service . . . and buy from me!

Of the three legs of the trilogy stool, marketing is without a doubt the most perplexing. In the first chapter it was discussed that business development was both an art form and a science. Nowhere in this business development process is that more obvious than in the marketing arena. Many marketing experts will tell you that this segment consists of much more science these days than art form. And they are right. There is an equal number that will swear it's more art than science. And they too are right. Regardless, there is no argument that marketing is a mysterious animal that has a multitude of intricate moving parts. But remember that we

---

10. Robert Bartels, *The History of Marketing Thought* (MN: Grid, Inc., 1976).

seem to have this ingrained need to complicate things. The more complicated, the better.

Again, it is quite simple when you keep it in perspective. You must qualify and understand who you are trying to reach. This is what you must remember:

 The basic premise of B2B marketing is to deliver the message of value the company or service provides to the "qualified" masses.

Qualified. That's the key. To as many "qualified" potential customers as our budget will allow, through the most effective means possible. Websites, chat rooms, TV, radio, social media, billboards, newspapers, email campaigns, texts, phone calls, handouts, direct mail, trade shows, or even those little "A-frame" things that folks wear and walk up and down the side of the highway to draw customers into a new pizza shop, are all means to market a product or service. Companies must determine the best tools or venues for what they are selling and who they want to sell it to. If a potential client is interested in your service or product, companies must also know where they typically go to investigate. What media or venue do they use to learn more about you? One of the worst mistakes we can make is to focus our advertising on trade periodicals that are only looked at by our peers. What are our potential clients reading? That's where we should market.

And what do we mean by "qualified?" Look at it as a math equation:

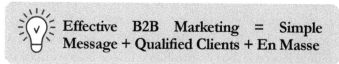 **Effective B2B Marketing = Simple Message + Qualified Clients + En Masse**

In the 60s, the Coppertone Suntan Lotion Company used a small light aircraft to fly up and down the beach at Coney Island in the summertime. It would tow a banner behind, showing a little girl with a dog, pulling on her swimsuit, revealing untanned, exposed skin that was at risk of getting sunburned. The tagline read, "Tan . . . Don't Burn, Use Coppertone." Direct marketing—a simple message to highly qualified customers, en mass. I would say that was a pretty good example of a qualified campaign.

In the 90s, when I first became involved with marketing and delivering our message to potential clients, the challenge was not nearly as complex as it is today. We developed TV ads, radio ads, direct mail pieces, collateral print brochures, VHS video tapes (yes, VHS), and full-page advertisements in magazines and periodicals. The internet was brand new, and only a handful of companies even had a website. Even though I worked for a Fortune 100 firm, our website was very rudimentary and read-only stuff. Most smaller B2B companies did not even have one.

We placed a lot of emphasis on personal client meetings, networking events, conventions, and trade shows. Some of our best partner clients and largest contracts came from relationships made at trade shows or conventions. Things have changed a lot since then, however. So, what is the best way to share or "market" our value? As a B2B company, that depends enormously on what you are selling and who you are trying to reach.

WHY IS MARKETING SO IMPORTANT?

Marketing has evolved into quite an amazing phenomenon. This is especially true in consumer-based marketing. Companies like Google, eBay, Wayfair, and Amazon have literally reinvented the way products and services are marketed and sold, and quite frankly, most of this data engineering is way over my head. It is said that roughly 46 percent of all consumer purchases today are done via smartphones or handheld devices, especially with the millennials, generation Y, and gen Z segments.

Given this fact, the way marketing is executed has metamorphosized into a new age of digital transactions. The enormous amount of information that is captured by companies today is off the charts.

 By tracking what we buy, what we look at on the internet, our tweets, our email traffic, our age, sex, race, viewing preferences, occupation, and personal profile information, these companies can now determine what we want to buy as consumers even before we do.

Have you ever searched on the web for something, say new tires, and the next time you go to your favorite gossip site, like MSN.com, there are ten different tire ads in the right margin? Is it magic? Maybe Big Brother? The power of these digital marketing tools is mind-boggling to say the least.

In an episode of the CBS program *60 Minutes*, it was said that the 2016 presidential election was tremendously influenced by digital social media marketing tools. There were some comments that I thought were quite humorous. The basic premise of the message was: *It was liberals that created social media tools like Facebook and Twitter, but it was the conservatives that figured out how to use them to win the election.*

We have yet to truly realize the full power of these tools as they continue to evolve and grow in power. The future of digital marketing is like the "Wild West." Beware.

Earlier we mentioned the importance of qualified masses. We have the ability now to collect unlimited data and information of almost any imaginable sort and execute marketing messages with surgical precision. If a company only wants to target white females in Tucson that drive four-wheel-drive vehicles, listen to jazz music, and drink Diet Coke, that target list can be produced and purchased. Now that is "qualified" at its finest. Frightening, I know, but quite true. We have come a long way from the Agora marketplace of ancient Athens. Using this ability to qualify email campaigns and focused advertising is a real advantage for our marketing efforts. Use it to your advantage where it makes sense.

In the past, marketing was about the creatives and the artists. The future of marketing is going to be about data scientists, information analysts, and software engineers. To survive, we must embrace this change. Great companies either change, or they die. John Maxwell said that great leaders have one thing in common: they see things before others see them. I strongly believe that applies to great marketers as well.

B2B MARKETING IS DIFFERENT

In B2B marketing, typical sales are geared toward longer and milestone-related sales cycles. In lieu of marketing a new cell phone that consumers might impulse buy at the retail store or online, B2B marketers find themselves creating content to support industrial machinery that could be as much as one million dollars or sharing project experience and performance history data to support the construction of a new sports arena worth five hundred million dollars.

 Before a client will make that kind of investment decision, they must be sure that the company and its talent—as well as the product or service—is the best choice. That is a process, not an impulse.

42

Before the rise of the internet and social media, the B2B marketer's job was easier. Marketing consisted mainly of creating and providing brand messaging and sales collaterals,[11] performing public relations and advertising, and organizing trade shows and other sales events. For the most part, the B2B sales team found and developed their own leads through referrals and connections, golf outings and partnering meetings, participating in trade organizations, or by just good ol' cold calling. For large, significant purchases or projects, a salesperson would spend months educating the buyer and developing the case for the purchase. They understood that they had to develop a relationship of trust and provide the right information at the right time within the buying process.

But given the advent of the internet, the behavior of B2B buyers has changed much like that of consumers, just not as much. This change has led to an evolution in B2B marketing tactics, making the B2B marketing function much more important to the B2B business development process than ever. Why? The reason is that, typically, the marketing group has a stronger skill set in data management and social media manipulation than sales, and without marketing leading the front-end process for the entire business development (BD) team, efficiency would suffer greatly.

The truth is, B2B marketers today assume much of the responsibility for client education, providing data and the relationship building that salespeople used to have to do face to face. They're using data-driven methods to identify qualified leads, provide information they need, then determine the exact and best way to support sales and customer service. This has made the process much more focused and concise, allowing customer-facing people like sales to be more effective. This requires interactive and timely

11. Traditional collaterals are printed material such as brochures, postcards, handouts, catalogs, white papers, newsletters, and equipment data sheets. Digital collaterals can be PDFs on a website or any material converted into digital format.

communication between marketing, sales, and customer service and is one of the primary reasons that these three groups *must* be players on the same coach's team.

The main point here is that the internet and the digital marketplace are both powerful and dangerous. Is all this instantaneous communication and personal information availability good or bad for our society? It will be decades before we can answer that question, but one thing is for certain:

 Marketing your firm and being present in this digital world is what we call a "no brainer." Do not get left behind.

Why is marketing so important? Because no matter how good your products may be or how qualified your people may be, if that message is not delivered or made available for clients to discover, huge growth simply cannot occur. Marketing is to the masses. Sales is one on one. For that growth to happen, these two segments have got to help each other. They must work as one.

WHAT SHOULD MY COMPANY DO?

Don't feel alone or get too overwhelmed at this point. All this philosophy and information about marketing is important and interesting, and as we have said, there are thousands of skilled consultants, books, and educational materials created on this subject. I would encourage any company that does not have a marketing expert in house to seek the advice of a credible source with experience in your specific field of business in order to help with the plan development phase that will be discussed later. Understand that the complexity and science we have outlined so far in the consumer and retail arenas requires a lot of knowledge and skill, especially in the digital and data manipulation areas.

The good news is that, in the B2B space, most of those retail and consumer digital marketing tools are not quite as needed or effective.

 Unlike consumer marketing, the idea of B2B marketing is more steered toward developing creative content, educating the client, generating interest, and peaking awareness—not necessarily to convince someone to purchase on the spot.

Since most business-to-business sales are about people trusting people and the development of long-term relationships, the marketing efforts surrounding business development will be less data manipulation intensive. As one of the three basic pillars of the trilogy, marketing plays a crucial role in opening the door for the next step in the process of making a new client or expanding an existing one. Later in Part 2, we will outline the basic elements of any good B2B marketing initiative and what should be included.

FOCUS ON EXISTING TOO

This is going to make a lot of people cringe, but instead of spending all your marketing dollars and marketing energy on new customer acquisition, focus on expanding relations with existing clients. The key phrase is "customer retention," and we will talk more about why in Part 2. We are obsessed with new client growth in our marketing programs, but given that 80 percent of our revenue comes from existing clients, marketing should focus on them as well.

What things did you do that made people buy from you in the first place? Develop a program of 50/50 that re-emphasizes those things. Spend at least 50 percent of your marketing resources on existing clients. Put programs and marketing-related material in play designed to "thank" customers and send the message that you are grateful for their business. Spotlight a successful client business or project on your website or through an email campaign. Create customer forums or blogs and invite all your clients to participate and share ideas about your products and services. Send out rewards or special promotional ideas and programs. Be creative and inclusive of your existing client base.

We will talk about this repeatedly throughout the text, for good reason.

 Focusing on existing clients with the same amount of zeal as we use to track down new ones is a power point and a differentiator for any company.

Most do not, and if your company embraces this one simple idea, you will be ahead of the pack.

BRAND AND CULTURE

What is your brand? Your brand is not your logo. Your brand is not a catchy slogan. Your brand is not your website.

 Your brand is not who YOU just say you are. **Your brand is who you really are and what you do and why you do it.**

It is what *others* say you are. It is your trust—your bond. It is also what you are known for in the marketplace.

Even though we live in a world with over seven billion people, you would be surprised how small most B2B marketplaces can be. People (competitors and clients alike) know each other; they talk and share experiences and war stories. When people talk about your firm, are they talking about quality work or cheapest price? What are people saying about your company? The marketing team sets the pace and the standard for delivering this company brand. Your brand is the reputation of the company. Develop it, nurture it, and protect it.

What do you want clients to see when they look at your company? Marketing must work with the other groups (sales and customer service) to humanize the brand and influence how the brand is used. The marketing team must be the best steward of the brand possible, but the real brand is the personality of the collective. As a young man at Federal Express, my blood ran "purple and orange." I felt that Federal Express was the greatest company on the planet. What kind of message did I convey to everyone I encountered?

The key to any successful brand is the culture your employees work in every day. Italian philosopher Niccolò Machiavelli wrote a paper in the 1500s that encouraged "the end justifies the means" behavior, especially among politicians. Someone that is known as Machiavellian is "sneaky, cunning, and lacking a moral code."[12] What is your company culture? Machiavellian or encouraging?

It has been said many times that culture eats strategy for breakfast. What does that mean? What that means is we can develop the most well-thought-out, expensive, and ideal strategic plan possible to grow the business, but if the culture at our company is not aligned with the strategy, the outcome can be disastrous. Employees are the lifeblood of any firm. The culture and work environment matter more than anything else, and when employees are willing to leave

---

12. Vocabulary.com, keyword: *Machiavellian*.

for a very small increase or possibly take a pay cut to work in an environment they like, the company loses enormously.

If the company culture is not healthy and employees do not feel the love, then what are they conveying to clients? Sadly, the vast majority of all companies think they have a great culture and employees are happy, when in fact, it is quite different than they imagine.

Creating or stimulating a company culture isn't just having jeans day or a ping pong table. Those are perks, not culture.

 Culture isn't what you do but how you do it and how you live your mission statement.

The culture of the company is the personality of a company. It defines the environment in which employees work and how employees feel and speak about the company— what is encouraged or discouraged, or what is acceptable or unacceptable in the company. Does the company have a culture of fear or inclusion? While strategy is determined by the strategic plan, culture is the blend of the leadership vision and the knowledge and experiences of employees.

One of the saddest things in business development (BD) is when the elements are in place for real explosive growth within a small established B2B company, but a "dinosaur" or outdated culture riddled with paradigms exists within the leadership team, creating a negative culture that is transmitted through the employee conduit to existing and future clients.

 Leadership sets the culture, and no level of marketing, sales, or customer service effort can overcome a negative culture.

PUBLIC RELATIONS

What is public relations (PR)?

 Public relations:

an intentional messaging process that fosters beneficial relationships between companies, organizations, and their clients.[13]

Mutually beneficial relationships are the desired result and key building blocks of any B2B marketing effort. The preceding definition does not say that public relations is a person. It is a process. Public relations is one of the most important processes in business development marketing. Of the four simple truths outlined earlier in the introduction of this book, trilogy truth number four speaks to this very well. Let's restate these four simple truths of business development:

1. Business development is a team sport.

2. Business development is both an art form and a science.

3. Business development is a concept, *not a department!*

4. Business development is an endeavor that *must* be mutually beneficial.

Trilogy truth number four states that endeavors must be mutually beneficial! Mutually beneficial for whom? For any relations of any kind to work, it must be mutually beneficial for both sides. Some call it a win-win. Public relations is the way companies do this with targeted customers to create and maintain a positive image and develop a strong relationship with potential clients. Getting out in the community, providing resources on a Habitat for Humanity project, providing

---

13. Author's paraphrase.

funding for a community event, hosting educational events, or even offering to provide free services to earn trust are all great methods of PR.

Advertising is creating content to be promoted through different media venues, but public relations is a strategic communication process that builds mutually beneficial relationships with people and organizations.

 Knowing how to wisely execute and build public relations within the markets you pursue is pivotal to the growth strategy.

The best companies always embrace PR as a keystone tool.

B2B PRODUCTS VERSUS PROFESSIONAL SERVICES

Does the marketing team have a clear understanding of what are you selling? Even though the trilogy concepts are universal in the B2B world, there will be a significant difference in marketing tactics depending upon whether you are selling products or services. Is one more difficult than the other? Not more difficult, just substantially different.

Products

A product is a tangible thing, an item you can touch. It can be small like a new pump, or it can be huge like a new D8 Caterpillar Bulldozer. You can go to a website and see a picture along with detailed specifications, or you can go to a dealer and drive one. The following are some good examples:

- Industrial machinery
- Manufacturing of anything
- Medical devices and equipment

- Electrical switchgear
- Pumps and motors
- Fleet cars
- Aircraft parts
- HVAC parts
- Office furniture

Some of these are very well suited to be sold online, and some are not. There are a million examples on the internet of great B2B product websites and apps, and if you do sell B2B products, website sales are and will be a huge part of your marketing strategy. The marketing team could employ consumer tactics and might develop sites for people to buy anything from HVAC parts to used construction equipment.

Marketing smaller products in the B2B space is a little more like consumer and retail. With small product marketing, the marketing and customer service segments of the BD team *must* be totally in sync and firmly aligned organizationally. Larger B2B products and services marketing is not as likely to totally happen online. For someone to purchase a $250,000 liquid-filled transformer for a municipal utility or six hundred new golf carts for Pebble Beach, trust and people are going to have to be involved.

Professional Services

Marketing professional services is more difficult because there is no tangible product, and as we have stressed, relationships are an even bigger key to success.

Professional services include venues such as,

- Architectural and engineering design
- Construction and project management
- Accounting and legal
- Consulting (marketing, advertising, business services, etc.)

Professional service marketers must anticipate and understand the tactics required to provide the level of information and experience that will be needed to build loyalty and trust.

But regardless if you are in professional services or product marketing, after your media has delivered the experience or evidence of your qualifications, the process still falls back to client trust and requires that people from both sides (the company and the client) begin the courtship process to closure. Remember:

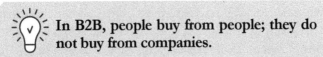 **In B2B, people buy from people; they do not buy from companies.**

There are basic marketing concepts at the core of both products and professional services, and you must understand what you are selling and to whom you are speaking to best structure your marketing strategy.

COMMUNICATION: THE FACE OF THE COMPANY

"Marketing communication" (MarCom) is an industry buzz phrase that is described as all the messages and media your company may deploy to communicate with potential clients and the market in general. The MarCom message should be owned by the marketing team but developed by all three segments. There are a variety of methods of marketing communication that include the following:

- Advertising
- Personal interactions

- Direct marketing campaigns (email, direct mail, web banners, etc.)
- Public relations
- Sponsorships, events, and conventions

But the message that is developed about the company and the way it is communicated to and perceived by potential clients is owned by marketing. Marketing should understand the arena in which your company is engaged, from customer's needs to analysis of topics to social media and search methods. Marketing must be the group that considers what and how the image, content, message, and overall customer experience is delivered.

Marketing must be the champion of the message that becomes the initial part of the customer experience. Why are you in business? What is in it for any potential client that trusts your company? These are the messages that marketing is charged with carrying to the world. Communicating that message effectively and clearly in the best way for your specific market is key to overall success.

MARKETING TOOLS AND COLLATERALS

How does the business development team get the company message of value, culture, brand statement, and product information delivered to the market? What tools and methods should be used? These are very important questions to be considered.

 Marketing tools are methods, strategies, and actions that marketing uses to deliver and promote that message of value for your products or services.

There are so many different tools, so I am not going to try to create an exhaustive list. Let us touch on a few basic tools that have shown the most effective return for effort in a B2B setting.

Website

It goes without saying that the company website may be the most important tool in the arsenal. Whenever anyone anywhere suggests, talks about, or even mentions a company, *what is the first thing a person always does?* Google them, of course!

 Science suggests that people make their mind up about the worth of that company in roughly ten to fifteen seconds.

That's not much time to make a good first impression. Make it count.

If your company sells products, then the website may also be your catalog and order portal. The key to any good website is ease of use, ease of navigation, look & feel, and clarity. When someone engages the company website, it should be immediately obvious what the company does. The client should not have to figure it out. With a limited marketing budget, most successful firms choose to invest a larger portion of available resources into the website than any other tool. It is the first impression point of contact and has proven to be the most important tool to date.

Social Media

Social media is arguably the most versatile and cost-effective marketing strategy that B2B businesses can use to reach their target audience. Well over 95 percent of B2B marketing teams are using social media to reach their new and existing customers. According to a recent study, 71 percent of the U.S. population has at least one social media profile, and estimates predict that in just a few years, the number of worldwide social media users will reach about 3.02 billion people.[14] Wow. That's powerful.

So, why should you care?

- Most of your customers are on social media.

- Some clients will be more receptive to your message on social media.

- Marketing through social media can help increase brand recognition.

- Website traffic can be stimulated by social media.

- Various social media outlets reach different clients. (Facebook is for one target, LinkedIn for another.)

- Social media advertising allows you to target and retarget.

- By posting content that is interesting or valuable, you are making your brand known and familiar for new and current customers.

 Social media is also very cost effective. The price is typically three to five times *less* expensive than advertising through traditional media.

If you are not active with social media, start now.

Brochures and Business Cards

Glossy slicks or black and white printed on a dot matrix printer? There are as many different opinions for collaterals

14. J. Clement, "Number of Social Media Users Worldwide from 2010 to 2021 (in Billions)," 2018. Retrieved from www.statista.com/statistics/278414/number-of-worldwide-social-network-users/.

(printed matter or digital client sharing information of any sort) as there are golf carts in Lee and Collier County, Florida! The main thing to remember about these items is that each should be simple and to the point. Pictures are always better than a ton of wordy text. Brochures are attention grabbers. If your product or service is such that technical specifications or detailed descriptions are needed, then by all means, create a secondary sheet with all that boring detail. Do not try to combine the two, because one document cannot be both. Your audience will dictate which document (or both) needs to be used.

Brochures should also be designed as "leave behinds" not "lead withs." B2B business development is about people earning the trust of other people in the right way. Handing out equipment data sheets or a handful of brochures before you even know anything about the "pain" or issues you might be able to solve is like a doctor prescribing medicine before he or she has ever examined the patient. I cannot tell how many young BD folks I have worked with that feel the need to sit down, open the brochure, and start reading it to potential clients!

 70 percent of all customers buy because they like, trust, and respect the salesperson.

Business cards are also quite diverse. Do we use portrait or landscape design? Color or black and white? Do we print on both sides? How much information should be on the card? What about digital cards that can be shared or transferred by my device? It is really a cultural and personal preference thing. Having a convenient way to provide your contact data for future reference is the goal, but I have always found that simpler is better. Keep in mind that if you are an accounting firm, then a highly creative, colorful, "talking" digital card may be a bit much. Conversely if you are a marketing or advertising consultant, then the client may be expecting a little more pizazz.

Proposals

Proposals are a staple in any B2B marketing and sales effort and are the next step in the winning process. Unlike brochures that are typically general in nature, proposals are very specific, targeted at the "pain points" of a unique need or project. You cannot develop a proposal until the salesperson has listened to the needs and developed a solution.

When developing proposals, the best rule of thumb is to try and customize them to the fullest extent possible. Some proposals are a direct response to a request for proposals (RFP) or a request for qualifications (RFQ) provided by the client. These typically have a very defined set of submittal instructions and *must* be followed to the letter. This is most prevalent in public offerings, bidding, or submissions.

If the proposal is private and not public in nature, then including customized items on the cover page of the proposal such as,

- client's name or company logo (if reproducing the logo is allowable)
- specific service or product offered
- project name and location
- brief executive summary description of the solution offered in a title or summary block

... shows the care, time, and thought that has gone into the development of that proposed solution. Try and avoid generic proposals that feel mass produced. With today's digital marketing tools, inserting this type of customized information is really quite easy. This added step is what will set your proposal apart from others.

One thing to keep in mind about proposals is this: Many companies think that subscribing to a service that notifies them weekly of all RFQs and RFPs coming out, watching a series of websites, or being on some sort of bid list, then simply creating a proposal and "throwing it in the mix" along with hundreds of others, is business development. It is not. This is what is known as *proposal roulette*. Every once in a while you might get lucky, but the odds are tremendously stacked against you.

Submitting a proposal for a sale is a wonderful thing. But as we have said, regardless if it is a private client or a government agency, people still buy from people. If the receiver of your proposal has never met you or your business development team and never heard of your company, then you have two chances: slim and none.

However, business development teams that create relationships with potential proposal recipients in advance typically are the ones that win. I know there will be tons of people that read this and cringe, and even though our public bidding process strives to be fair and impartial, the reality is that it's simply not. People are involved in the selection, and people want to buy from people they know, respect, and trust. Get out there and get known.

Advertising

This may be the oldest tool in the history of marketing and should be a staple in your business development strategic plan. Advertising comes in millions of forms: magazines, newspapers, and periodicals of all sorts, billboards, T-shirts, banners, giveaways, logos on the side of the company trucks, TV, and radio. Then there is the insane world of online advertising. Good luck.

The primary thought here again is simple: clarity and focus. A couple of months ago I watched a TV commercial for a product called Rogaine. It was a great commercial with an older couple, smiling and holding hands and such. But after the thirty seconds was up, I had absolutely no idea what Rogaine did. After seeing the same commercial a few times, I went to the internet and did some research to find out it was for hair loss! Really? If the client cannot determine from your ad what you do and how it will help them, then the advertisement has failed miserably.

Presentations

Another time-tested marketing tool is the presentation. Back in the 80s, the marketing creative team would make printed transparencies to be used on an overhead projector, or sometimes they created slides to be put into a slide carousel and projected on a screen. Try dragging a carousel full of slides and a projector through the airport sometime! They would also create printed and bound copies to hand out so everyone could follow along during the presentation. Giving presentations was quite an undertaking.

Then along came Microsoft and the software PowerPoint. We had died and gone to heaven. Even today, although there are several other presentation applications like Prezi that are great, PowerPoint is still the workhorse. Presentations are necessary, important, and key pieces of the marketing and sales arsenal. The most important thing to remember is the same as the other tools: Keep it simple and interesting to look at, and use more pictures than text.

 If you want to glaze over a room full of potential clients, fill up each slide with small text and read each line to them.

Remember the three rules of giving any presentation:

1. Tell them what you are going to tell them.

2. Tell them.

3. Then tell them what you told them.

Good sales presentations, either in person or in the form of a webinar, are short and concise, and the text is in "talking point" form as an overview or a guide for the audience to glance at while they listen to the speaker. Given that the marketing team is typically much more creative and capable of much better content, salespeople should let these be developed and maintained by the marketing professionals, if possible. Collaboration on content, length, and visual appeal from all three trilogy groups is the best overall approach.

The exception is if the speaker is delivering a white paper or technical presentation. These highly effective marketing presentations are expected to be detailed and comprehensive. That's what makes them so effective. Even generic presentations sometimes are a must, depending on the unique situation.

 But to know and understand the target audience and create presentations that are targeted, focused, specific, applicable, and relevant to the group, is always, always the best approach.

Events and Associations

Hosting, attending, and participating in events and associations has historically been a staple in marketing any B2B company. Over the past few years, there seems to be a feeling that we are moving away from these personalized, face-to-face activities and that online and digital interactions are replacing them. To think like that is a strategic mistake. In my opinion, this venue is making a comeback and will be a significant and key resource for B2B business development in the future. As more and more marketing is done digitally, the personal element will erode, making clients long for interaction with real human beings. Teams that embrace this now and participate in such events will be in the top 10 percent of successful marketers in the future. Make it part of your plan now.

The U.S. Bureau of Labor Statistics expects conventions and event planning jobs to grow at a rate that exceeds the average for all other occupations in the coming years.[15] Tradeshows, association meetings, technical conferences, "lunch and learn" seminars, and your own company-sponsored events give BD people the opportunity to meet clients, listen to their needs, and begin a relationship of trust. That can only be done face to face.

As I have said, presentations are powerful, personal, and highly effective ways to deliver your message to a single client or an entire conference room. Along these same lines, two of the most powerful business development tools are (1) the delivery of a technical white paper or (2) being a subject matter expert speaker at a conference, trade show, or event. Although I still believe that the future will shift back towards in-person delivery, in today's digital marketplace, these time-tested tools can also be extended into the world of webinars, blogs, and online chat-related exchanges. Posting a technical white paper discussion forum in the form of a blog that stimulates conversation among interested technical parties is today's equivalent of that face-to-face conference, multiplied by ten thousand because of the exponential nature of the internet. Embracing both the personal event and the digital

15. "Meeting, Convention, and Event Planners," *Occupational Outlook Handbook,* from the Bureau of Labor Statistics, 2018. Retrieved from https://www.bls.gov/ooh/business-and-financial/meeting-convention-and-event-planners.htm.

event is the winning combination. Without question, some of the largest client contracts I have ever won have come from these types of venues. Being an expert and a solution provider attracts clients to your team like flies to honey. Encourage the sales and marketing teams to engage as many of these marketing events as financially possible.

CONCLUSION

As the first part of the trilogy, marketing is the front-end piece that opens the door in the process of making a loyal client. This area of focus can be deep and wide and involved, and there are many more elements to this complex science than we have discussed here. We have only touched the major segments. The power point here is that we must embrace the importance of marketing to the whole business development engine and ensure that our marketing team is engaged in the collaborative planning process and has the right tools needed to support both sales and customer service to ultimately best serve the client.

4.

SALES

Nothing happens until somebody sells something. (Henry Ford)

I have long thought that the most mystical, interesting, and exciting "leg" of the trilogy was sales. This is most likely because sales is my area of passion. The most wonderful feeling in the world as a B2B sales guy is that moment of truth during the "tag team" meeting (we will describe what that means in a moment) when your technical expert personally connects with the client's technical expert, and you can see the bond between them emerge like a warm sunrise. It is a wonderful thing.

Creating such a winning environment for both sides is mostly about the attitude of the salesperson. I have always said,

 Sales success is 15 percent technical and 85 percent attitude. You can teach technical, but you cannot teach attitude.

Everybody seems to loathe the salesman. Nobody wants to admit he or she is a salesman. In the technical world, when an engineer or a plant operator finds out you are a salesman for your firm, they instantly move you into the untrustworthy, incompetent, and "waste of skin" bucket. That is part of the reason that many technical salespeople prefer a different title like engineering consultant or technical solutions advisor.

The image of the "sales guy" has always been depicted this way. How many remember the TV program *WKRP in Cincinnati?* Dressed in polyester suits, with plaid shirts and lime green pants, Herb Tarlek was the radio advertising sales guy and routinely demonstrated that he was a moron and incapable of intellectual thought—aggressive, self-centered, stupid, deceitful, and certainly not to be trusted. Hollywood has burned this stereotype into our brains over the years, and we all have come to believe it.

Reality could not be farther from this image.

 Without someone out on the front lines, forging ahead, developing client relationships and tirelessly bringing in orders, there would be no reason for the critical functions that make up the core reason you are in business.

There would be no need for research and development, engineering, accounting, production, Six Sigma experts,[16] or shipping and receiving departments if somebody didn't sell something first.

In the opening overview, I was a little hard on the use of the term "business development manager." Allow me to apologize for being so aggressive toward all of us noble

---

16. "Six Sigma (6σ) is a set of techniques and tools for process improvement." Retrieved from https://en.wikipedia.org/wiki/Six_Sigma.

BDMs (business development managers). The truth of the matter is, what you call the folks in your organization that stand out front developing trust and bringing in relationships and business for your firm can be business development managers, client service advisors, or customer account managers. There are literally hundreds of combinations for this role. I still have people in my organization today that we call business development managers because of the perception issues discussed. Create and use the one you feel best suits your environment and delivers *your* company's message in the best light.

The power point here is that we need to remember that business development is not a title but a philosophy of unity. The people that you engage for this segment of the trilogy are the representatives and sellers of your product or service, no matter what you choose to call them.

Sales has been studied, analyzed, and reinvented at least a thousand times. There are vast teams of PhDs and scientists that study human behavior and delve into the psyche of the brain to unlock the mysteries of sales. Millions and millions have been spent by companies on this endeavor, desperately searching for the secret formula that gives their sales machine an edge. I must admit that many of them are extraordinarily successful. As with marketing, they follow our internet searches and pop-up stuff that we might be interested in and coerce us to buy. They design Facebook ads and TV ads and track our online buying habits and only show us the things we like. They know me better than I know myself. It's very frightening. They have turned a noble art form called "sales" into an obscure world of science, technology, and manipulation.

However, for all its stereotyping, misrepresentation, mystery, and difficulty . . .

Sales is what makes the world go around. Without it, we would not have the things we all enjoy today, and our personal worlds would be limited to what we could make, grow, or borrow on our own.

Hard to swallow, I know. But sales are crucial to the trilogy concept and to your business development engine.

TYPES OF SALES

In the world of business-to-business sales, there are many different scenarios that can constitute a sale. Services, products, consulting, airtime, internet space, advertising—the list goes on. But it has been my experience that there are only two basic *types* of sales ever made:

1. Wants
2. Needs

Subsequently it has also been shown that there are two basic categories of sales made:

1. Consumer-based
2. Business-based (commercial, industry, and government B2B/B2G)

There are obviously many more microcategories like retail, donations, online, discount, B2B, B2G, B2C, and so on, but for purposes of this point we will use the two basic sides of the coin: consumer and business.

Admittedly, I am not an expert in the retail/consumer sales arena, but a vast majority (some 80 percent) of most retail sales are wants based, not needs based.

Our personal devices are the best salesmen that the consumer space has ever known. We are consumers of things we don't really need, are we not? We buy things we do not need with money we do not have. Think back on the last fifty purchases that you or your spouse have made and count how many were truly needs. Now we are not talking about things we must have to live, like food or gas or essentials—these are things we need to survive. We are talking about purchases of things we do not *need*.

There is a local "doo-dad" emporium near where I live that my wife simply adores. I have noticed when we go in there that the "salespeople" know her and steer her to the items they sell that push her buttons. We always come out with things that she had not planned to buy. Similarly, boats are my passion. At the marine supply store I frequent, the guys in there know that I like gadgets. So whenever I go to get some lower unit fluid, I always seem to come out with a new depth finder.

Conversely, 80 percent of B2B sales are needs based, and the remaining 20 percent are wants based. At work, when was the last time you noticed them replace a perfectly good desk chair or buy a new company truck when the existing one was serving the company just fine? This doesn't really have a great deal of bearing on the trilogy concept, but understanding this distinction between B2B sales and consumer-based sales will help you develop your strategy. We will talk about that in Part 2.

No matter the type of sale, the role of salesperson is paramount to success or failure of any business development initiative. Without them, the stool would tip over. The success of the sales team determines the success of the entire company. Regardless of his or her job, every employee should help to preserve existing clients and work to find new ones.

Allow me to make it very simple. What is the common goal of any company?

> **Regardless of what product or service each is engaged in, every company, group, or organization, profit or non-profit, is selling or promoting something.**

I know, you are saying to yourself right now that I am wrong. *If we were Walmart or Macy's or selling used cars or cellular telephones, that would be very true. But my company is a non-profit food bank.* Or maybe, *I work at a public utility;* or how about, *I am in the U.S. Navy.* It is easy to see how one might think these types of organizations are different. But if you are truly honest, you would see that the food bank is promoting the concept that all human beings have the right to eat, and the utility is selling power. The Navy several years ago had a marketing slogan that said, *"It's not just a job, it's an adventure."* They were selling to a specific demographic (young and courageous Americans) the idea of being a part of protecting the greatest nation on Earth. Please understand that I am not trying to trivialize these honorable institutions; I am simply trying to demonstrate the idea that all organizations are selling something.

If you accept that single truth, then you already have a distinct advantage. The challenge is how we go about the pursuit of that common purpose and to what degree. For anyone or any company to be successful, they must understand and embrace this concept and grasp the idea that sales is part of an overarching business development concept, not an initiative of itself.

> **To sell is to listen and serve. When you talk, you are only repeating what you already know. But if you shut up and listen, you might actually learn something useful and meaningful.**

For years I have told salespeople that selling is about listening, not talking. In 2016 I was the leader of a new start-up division tasked with creating an industrial process group in a marketplace where we were an unknown. The director of that group under me was a wise and seasoned guy who had an enormous amount of experience in the specific market we were pursuing. His name was Steve Farmer, and he also happens to be a very dear friend. Chris Robinson, one of his managers, set up a meeting with a potential client, and we all were to meet for a casual introductory lunch.

Being the senior guy of the three, when we arrived, I told them both in the parking lot that sales was about listening and that I was not going to talk too much—and neither should they. We all agreed. When we got inside and sat down and began to chat, the aggressive, rookie sales guy in me came out, and it was like someone had put a quarter in me and pulled that handle. For the next forty-five minutes, I dominated the conversation, and the client could do nothing but eat and nod. When it was over and we all got back in the car, Steve turned to me in a delightfully calm voice and said, "So that was you not talking, huh?" We all died laughing. They still remind me of that every chance they get. Even the best of us forget the basics sometimes. We never got any work from that company.

Sales is not about walking in and dominating the conversation or presenting a slick brochure with hi-res glossies and regurgitating features and benefits. It's not about selling them what a salesperson may think they need or want them to buy before he or she even sits down with the client.

Another huge mistake many salespeople make is they "we we" on the customer:

- *We* have this or that product!
- *We* do that better than anyone else!
- *We* have ten thousand employees!
- *We* have offices in every country!

Who cares? Every company can produce a "we we" list. So what? For successful salespeople, the real commodity is trust. How do we serve them best and earn customers' or clients' trust? By listening to their "pain," understanding their needs, and helping them achieve their goals. When a great salesperson does that, they can then achieve their goal.

BILLIARDS

One of my favorite analogies is that selling is just like playing billiards. Sometimes you get to make that perfectly lined-up, straight-in shot to the corner. Nothing impeding the shot, plenty of space, yours to lose. If only everything was that easy. However, in most cases, sales is more of a "banked-in" shot. It requires that we bounce the shot off another ball or two and hit at least one bumper. These bumpers and balls represent asking for a referral from a contact; cross-selling to an existing client a service you provide that he or she didn't know you provided; helping someone for free, anticipating landing another piece of work or a totally new relationship.

There are a multitude of possible combinations, but the point is it takes finesse and tactical maneuvering talent to connect all the right dots. Really successful salespeople understand this, are always on the lookout for a bank shot, and have developed a finely-honed talent for being able to see three moves ahead.

TYPES OF SALES ROLES

The task of selling the products and services any B2B company offers typically falls to the sales staff or the designated team of people specifically chartered with bringing in revenue, regardless of what they are called. Many companies try to have one type of salesperson perform any and all these sales-related duties. In most cases, one size does not fit all. There are many different types of salespeople with very different talents and personality traits, serving a variety of functions. There is also a plethora of titles; here are just a few:

- Sales representative, sales executive, sales consultant
- Business development manager, business development director
- Technical sales consultants (medical, scientific, etc.)
- Sales engineer
- Relationship manager, consultant, client relationship manager
- Territory manager, territory account manager
- Account manager, key account manager, strategic account manager, major account manager
- Internal sales associate, Call Center operator, customer service representative

Some are highly technical in nature and are subject matter experts in the field they serve, like sales engineers and technical sales consultants. Others are usually more senior-level positions and are relationship developers and creators of opportunity, dealing with C-level clients and higher-level decision makers. Some are in the client maintenance mode. Each is equally key to the generation of revenue, and one is not necessarily more important than the other. But it is critical to understand that each plays a very different role in the organization, and each requires a different skill set.

 Having the wrong type of person in the wrong role usually means failure for that person and ultimately the sales team.

Salespeople are basically divided into two distinct categories: new development and maintenance. New business developers are the long sales cycle folks whose role is to prospect and cultivate new clients, new opportunities, new markets, and new venues for any product or service. These business developers are focused on growth, expansion of existing markets, and playing the part of advancing the strategic goals of the company vision. Sometimes they are part of a "tag team" (we will discuss that in a moment). These are more "consultant-type" people and the team members that deal with higher level clients and their needs and ideas.

The opposite of developers are the maintenance folks: account representatives, client relationship specialists, and key account managers. These professionals are not the same as business developers. Their role is typically to maintain and expand existing client relationships, and therefore the focus area for them is as much in support of the customer service pillar of the trilogy as it is sales. Keeping existing clients happy, taking orders and selling recurring products, solving daily problems, dealing with warranty issues and passive referrals, watching for critical needs from existing clients, and expanding relationships into new business is their mission. These roles should really report to customer service, not sales.

Not understanding these differences is a big area of failure in many sales organizations. Selling varies greatly depending upon the role the salesperson is playing and the product or service. I have at one time or another done them all. Equipment and gadgets are the easiest because the features and benefits are more obvious and often times will sell themselves. Services like construction, preventative maintenance, IT services, cleaning, and training are harder to sell because even though the client can see other successes, the outcome is still not certain.

Technical sales are unique because it does require the person to be a subject matter expert (SME) or at least have a SME as part of the tag team.

 But far and away, professional services like advertising, architecture design, financial services, engineering, accounting, and legal services are the hardest, because at the end of the day, you are selling human trust and intangible intellectual property.

This requires the client to have 100 percent faith in the unseen, uncertain outcome and the company team's ability to deliver.

THE TAG TEAM APPROACH

We have referred to the tag team a couple of times. Allow an explanation of what that means. I have said it hundreds of times: 85 percent of success in sales is due to that salesperson's personality and their ability to communicate, listen, negotiate, and offer solutions. Only 15 percent is a result of their technical ability. You can learn just about anything technical with enough time and focused study, but you can't learn personality. I have seen that proven time and time again. However, it is important that salespeople know the product or service.

Einstein said that if you can't explain it in simple terms, then chances are you don't understand it well enough. If you can't explain it, you don't need to be sharing it. It's perfectly OK as a salesperson to not be a subject matter expert, but you absolutely have got to know your limits and have a strong technical resource at your disposal.

Years ago, when I was a young business developer, I made a wonderful discovery. The company I worked for supplied huge mechanical rotating industrial machinery and total engineered systems into the industrial space. Big projects with lots of complicated science and engineered moving parts. I understood how the pieces worked and what made up these complex systems, but I didn't really have a very strong technical grasp of the intricacies of detailed design. You could say I was far from a subject matter expert.

I was maybe thirty years old at the time, and our chief engineer was a sixty-something Finnish man named Ossie. Ossie had worked in the industry for over forty years and was maybe the most knowledgeable person I have ever met on the types of systems that company designed. However, he wasn't exactly the best choice when it came to first impressions. But he liked me and would always make himself available if I was going to visit a client.

One day he told me something that has always stuck with me. He said, "If you will tee up the ball, I will drive it down the fairway." That tag team formula has worked in spades for years. I would go and visit with clients and listen to what their needs and pain issues were at the time. Sometimes I would know the solution and could structure a deal. But sometimes they would want to drill down technically into more detail than I could possibly answer. I would simply stop and say, "This is great, and you are asking really terrific questions. Unfortunately I am not the right guy to answer them. Would it be OK if I came back next Tuesday with our chief engineer? He can certainly answer these questions and provide any technical detail you may want to know." It never failed.

There are two takeaways from that example salespeople should *never, ever* forget.

1. *Never, ever* try and bluff someone if you do not know the answer. If people determine that you

are doing that, any chance at trust will evaporate immediately. Getting a second chance is near impossible.

2. It affords you the chance to make a second visit and be better prepared to create a client for life.

PROFESSIONAL SERVICES: SELLER DOER + AUGMENTATION

In B2B business development, most of what companies offer are tangible products and services, and the salespeople and tag teams we have discussed so far work great. The exception to this rule is a unique sales role in professional services called the "seller doer." This technique has been employed for the past one hundred years in what is called the *seller doer model*. What does that mean?

OK, let's just say you are an engineering company that only provides design services. You provide and sell intellectual property. People *are* the product. Ideas, knowledge, experience, solutions, designs, calculations, drawings, and project schedules are the deliverables to the client. In this world, it is all about selling trust and billable hours, and the amount of time an employee is "utilized" (or their utilization rate—UR) is the typical key metric and indicator of success.

There are exceptions, but for the most part, technical folks like engineers and accountants don't typically make very good salespeople. They will procrastinate and put it off and do everything else that needs to be done and put sales effort last. Trust me, I fully understand and appreciate why they are this way. For all the reasons they were drawn to the sciences of accounting and law and engineering, they repel from sales. But in order to win work or sell "product," they do it anyway.

The seller doer model is basically a two-step process.

1. Step one is the *seller part*. The engineer goes out and seeks a potential new piece of work from either an existing client or a new prospect. Once one is identified, a proposal or in some cases a qualifications document is submitted. If the client selects that proposal, then a purchase order or contract is awarded.

2. Step two is the *doer part*. The engineer then comes back to the office, begins the design, and engages in providing the absolute best product possible. After all, the reason they went to engineering school was because designing things and solving problems was their passion!

Given this scenario, let us make a couple of observations. First and foremost, this makes the sales cycle, at best, extremely cyclic (see *Figure 4*): feast or famine. When there is a big project to perform, everyone is busy, and nobody is out selling (note the four gray bars, with the space between indicating the time when one project ends and another one starts). As the project nears completion and the engineer begins to realize that in a few weeks they will be out of work, they get in the sales mode and run out to find another project—and the cycle repeats itself.

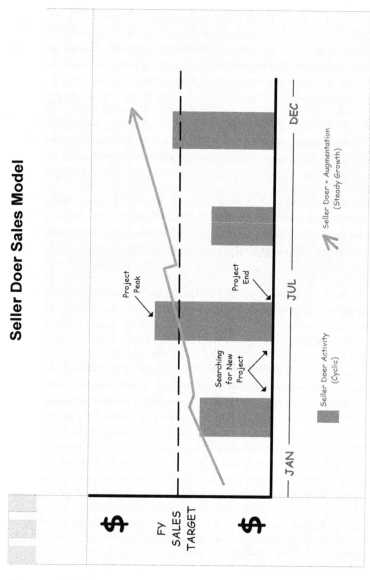

Figure 4: Seller Doer Sales Model

This is an oversimplification of a more complex marketplace, I know. But that is basically how it works and has worked for a very long time. Many terrific firms have been built this way, and even though it works, it does make aggressive business development growth very challenging.

In the past few years, however, some of the larger companies and a few more progressive small professional service firms have embraced what I call "augmentation." These firms have hired technical business developers that are full-time, technically minded individuals who are talented salespeople as well in order to "augment" the seller doer model. Their mission is to maintain relationships, keep abreast of activity in the sector or silo they are assigned, prepare proposals, and serve as liaison and sales coach to the team. They also develop new markets and prospect for new clients on an on-going basis. Usually these folks are part of a departmental or geographic team. Sometimes they are assigned to a silo, market, or sector.

 Regardless, the result of *seller doer + augmentation* is a smoothing out of the radical sales cycle and a more consistent and effective business development growth effort (note the arrow's steady growth from January to December).

ARE SALESPEOPLE BORN THAT WAY?

Do great salespeople have it ingrained in their DNA, or can just anyone become a *superstar?*

There are a lot of successful and prolific entrepreneurs out there with great ideas and coaching. One of my favorites is the founder of Herjavec Group, Robert Herjavec. You may have seen him on ABC's *Shark Tank* or read his book, *You Don't Have to Be a Shark*.[17] Great read. I highly recommend it. His personal story is amazing, and I find the ideas, feedback, and comments he gives to folks that come on the show totally unprepared to be spot on. Robert says that in order to be successful, everyone must be able to sell. That is almost an absolute in the universe. He also goes on to say that salespeople are not "natural born" and that anyone can become a good salesperson.

In January of 2017 Herjavec published a short piece called, "My 5 Essential Tips for Selling Anything to Anyone" that outlined some basic tips that are timeless. In general, they said something like this:

1. What you are really selling is you.

2. Shut up and listen.

3. Know who the decision makers are.

4. Understand what their pain points are.

5. Keep things simple.[18]

These could not be more accurate. They are ideas that we *all* should follow. I agree with him in concept that everyone can learn to sell. My experience has been that good techniques can and should be learned and practiced and that for anyone to be truly successful, they must be able to sell to some degree.

 Everyone is always selling something in life, whether it is themselves for a promotion or convincing their wives to buy a new fishing boat.

17. Robert Herjavec, *You Don't Have to Be a Shark: Creating Your Own Success* (NY: St. Martin's Press, 2016).

18. Robert Herjavec, "My 5 Essential Tips for Selling Anything to Anyone," 2017. Retrieved from www.robertherjavec.com/5-essential-tips-selling/.

By learning these habits, anyone can become a *good* salesperson. *Good*.

As I mentioned, Herjavec contends that good salespeople are not born that way and that anyone can be good at sales if they simply practice and focus and learn how. It is true that anyone can develop solid sales habits and techniques—and they should. He is right: some of the things that can be learned are sales pipeline management, time management, sales and business acumen, product/service knowledge, and sales forecasting. However, I must respectfully disagree with him on one very important point:

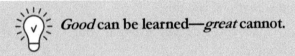

Good can be learned—*great* cannot.

It has been my experience that the great salespeople I have seen over the years do have a certain DNA or specific type of personality that gives them an advantage, and they possess traits that cannot be learned. You have met these types of people, I am sure. When they walk into a room, people migrate towards them. They have a God-given talent for making people feel comfortable. They have a warm and friendly personality that exudes both confidence and humility. They genuinely listen in order to understand the root cause of a company's real concerns or someone's personal pain and then offer winning solutions. These types think strategically. They are neither ashamed nor afraid at just the right moment to ask for the business.

Here are seven hard-to-learn personality traits to look for in great salespeople:

1. Strategic thinker; always looking to connect the dots

2. Integrity and honesty

3. The ability to hear "no" as an opportunity

4. Natural ability to listen—really listen for the unspoken issues

5. Talent for building rapport and earning trust

6. Confidence and drive to win; goal oriented

7. Humility and self-awareness

Sales is about solving problems. Not your problems but someone else's, and there are simply some people that are better at it than others. Some people are just going to be better at sales than others because of their natural talents. Finding them can be a challenge.

IS RELATIONSHIP SALES OBSOLETE?

Wow. I can't believe I asked that question. But the truth is, I have had it asked of me a lot. Believe it or not, there is a large contingent of younger B2B sales folks these days that use texts, email, tweets, and other digital tools to prospect and try to "ask for the business" without ever looking someone in the eye. Really. This new age of technology and global, instant communication is an awesome thing.

 Being connected and able to share things like quotations, proposals, drawings, letters of interest, contracts, pictures, and video with anyone, anywhere, instantly, has made doing business so much easier and faster.

There is no doubt that as these media improve, it will even get better. I embrace it fully. However, there will never be any substitute for building trust through human interaction. I have said this over and over that people buy from people. I certainly do when it really matters. Do you? If your career or your company's future depended upon ensuring that you picked the right equipment, vendor partner, or tax consultant, would you really want to choose that firm from some texts or tweets or even a Skype sales call? No, you would not.

Allow me to share a personal experience with real estate. The truly successful agents are the ones that have the ability to listen, empathize, and watch out for the client's best interests and make their clients feel like they are the only client in the world. With the millions of real estate search sites and homes listed, with thousands of photos and detailed descriptions, consumers are being made to feel like they can search for and buy real estate without ever leaving their kitchen table. And you can, no question. If the buyers know the area in which they are buying well—the surrounding political issues, good or bad, amenities and infrastructure performance, and if the area is growing or degrading—then it's a reasonably good bet they could find something that meets their needs and desires. But for most folks, a house will be the largest, most significant purchase they will ever make, and their financial future depends on making the best choice.

Also, most buyers are not experts in real estate law or finance. With a purchase of this magnitude, to have guidance from a sales or BD person who can be trusted makes the buyer's risk go down tremendously. Great agents listen to you and make you feel like you have 100 percent of their attention. They demonstrate that they really care about finding just the right place and that any major pitfalls are addressed. We are not talking about the salespeople who are fake, who pretend they care when they don't just to make a sale—I detest those types. But the agents that really do care about the outcome of your purchase, that you get the best value for your family, and that you're happy with the outcome. They understand the time-tested axiom:

 I will get what I want by helping you get what you want.

Recently my wife and I engaged a realtor/broker in Florida to help us find a vacation home. We picked a community we wanted to buy into and were given the name of a realtor by the community manager. We called this person and set up a time to meet. She had picked some places for us to look at, and we spent half a day riding around, looking at terrific places and talking. We picked a couple we liked and told her we were going to give it some thought and get back to her.

I am the kind of buyer that doesn't want to pay sticker price for anything—it's just my nature. So we wanted to make an aggressive offer and negotiate. Our realtor was immediately put off and distant. She said that this was a "hot" market and if we were not ready to buy right now and pay market price, we would most likely not find anything and would be a waste of her time. We fired her promptly.

By sheer coincidence, we were introduced to another agent in the area. We asked her to help us, and she seemed more than happy to listen. During the process she was patient, caring, took time to understand what we wanted, worked very hard to help us find our dream place (it took a year), and ultimately earned our trust and became a friend. We did find just the right property in the exact place we wanted and have told everyone we know about her and will do so from now on. If you buy or sell in SW Florida, you are crazy if you don't at least reach out to Paula Towell. She built client loyalty with us for life.

When a major B2B need arises and the client's reputation is at risk, they want the ability to look the salesperson in the eye and *know* that they can be trusted and that they care. "No relationship" sales is not obsolete and never will be. You might buy a new toaster online without any human contact, but no one will ever build a new hospital or a new airport or agree to buy a fleet of delivery trucks without human trust being involved.

If your sales team is not building personal relationships and client loyalty, then you are going to lose.

THE 86ᵀᴴ PERCENTILE

Have you ever worked with someone or managed someone that was charged with selling your products and services that seemed to have the DNA of a salesperson, was energetic and technically competent, but just never seemed to be able to get anything closed or sold? Everybody just loved this person, and they all said, "That girl has got to be in sales! She is a natural!" But then when it came down to it, she never seemed to be able to sell anything.

Well it's certainly not his or her fault that they aren't closing the deals, and it's not as uncommon as you might think. Not everyone is cut out to be a rainmaker. Not everyone is cut out to be a movie star or a brain surgeon either. That doesn't make them bad or good people, it simply means that God made us all unique and with an individual purpose. Think about it, how great would a baseball team really be if all nine players were only good at pitching?

Why did this person we all thought would be a superstar salesperson fail? Well one reason is that, although they are great with people, technically competent, never meet a "stranger," or have a wonderful ability to public speak, they are not salespeople by nature . . . they are public relations.

Public relations is a noble and needed profession. There is a very key role for public relations in our marketing strategy, as we have already pointed out. Without great public relations skills, people like politicians, talk show and news media types, and even your doctor breaking the news that you need a gallbladder operation, would be much less effective and comforting. The information that is being delivered could be painful or frightening if not presented in a right manner. Public relations is both needed and noble.

Public relations, however, is not to be confused with sales. A vast majority of the folks you will put on your sales team are in fact great public relations people.

 The first 85 percent of relationship sales (which *is* what great business development is all about) is in fact all about public relations.

Making a good first impression, building rapport, listening, asking questions, offering ideas, connecting the dots, and ensuring the right people from your firm are engaged are critical to success.

However, the second part of that equation and *by far the most difficult part* is the last 15 percent: sensing when the time is right, then asking for the business or the purchase order, offering a contract, getting to "yes," and closing the deal.

 Moving from the 85th to the 86th percentile in this process is the single most difficult thing for any salesperson to achieve.

Only about 10 percent of the salespeople I have ever managed, coached, or worked with have this natural ability. I am not sure why so many stumble at this point, but I have watched it for years. As we pointed out, many of these 85 percenters can *learn* to be closers, and I have coached quite a few to success and seen some good salespeople developed in this way. But the naturals are not as common as many believe and are very hard to spot. In the years that I have been hiring and managing salespeople, I have been wrong more than once. When you do find one of these 86 percenters, you have found a gem and should go to great lengths to retain them.

People have different skills and talents. Einstein said, "Everybody is a genius at something. But if you judge a fish by its ability to climb a tree it will live its whole life believing that it is stupid." Likewise, the business development organization will require specific talents for specific roles in all three pillars. The marketing team needs a unique skill set, as does the customer service group and the sales force. Regardless of the reason, when we are building our BD team, we must be vigilant to ensure that we choose the right team members for the right roles.

BEWARE OF WHALE HUNTERS

Anyone that knows me knows that I love metaphors and analogies to make points. Allow me to share two of my favorite ones. One of the greatest detriments to the success of the entire business development team is *whale hunters*. Whale hunters in the sales world are people who only want to find and close the "once in a lifetime" super deal—typically because they are selfish and mainly focused on the commission check involved. They fail to realize that most really successful companies are winners because they embrace multiple smaller wins and get blessed with that "whale" occasionally. If you are concerned about feeding your family, you would first focus on the abundant smaller fish in the shallow water rather than going out and searching for whales every day.

To use another metaphor, great sales team members realize that not only is this a team sport, but baseball games are won with base hits, not just home runs. Swinging for the fence every time one gets to bat is actually very self-centered.

The moral of these metaphors is that great salespeople know how to pursue both small and large opportunities and how to balance their time on both.

If the monthly sales quota is $500,000, for example, then finding ten, $50,000 sales opportunities is just as effective as finding one, $500,000 opportunity—and the smaller ones are typically a lot easier too. It also provides for diversity in the event that the one "whale" goes sour.

Trust me, as a selfish sales guy, if I had my choice, I would much rather be on the bow with a harpoon in my hand and all eyes on me than in the back of the boat with a cane pole and a cricket. But we must understand that the team mission is to consistently meet sales expectations, ensure the financial health of the company, and provide for its employees that rely on the business development team to bring in business. Team members that allow ego and false pride to prevail, ignoring the smaller opportunities and insisting on only spending their time hunting for "whales," may be hurting more than helping.

 Balance and perspective are the key. Great salespeople have the ability to recognize this and pursue both with equal zeal.

PROSPECTING AND "RULE 122"

The effort or initiative to find and win new clients is called *prospecting*. Prospecting is the process of identifying potential customers, then systematically communicating with them through a variety of ways in order to convert them from potentials to loyal clients.

There are so many different variations on how this has been done over the years that there would be no way to cover them all. Methods change, and the tools used have evolved and vary from industry to industry. What works in the service industry may not be applicable in a product sales environment. The constant, however, is prospecting as a task. It is really not complicated, but there are some basics.

Prospecting requires the salesperson to make what is referred to as "calls." Prospecting calls can be in person, on the phone, or through a variety of digital methods. Although there are a multitude of techniques, calls basically come in only a couple of forms.

Asking for referrals from existing clients or some other credible source, in any way, is known as a *warm call.* Unlike cold calls, warm calls occur when there is some sort of prior or pre-established connection with the potential client. Warm call potentials can come from places like,

- colleagues and referrals from clients
- people we know from another venue
- people who have responded to an advertising campaign
- people that filled out a survey
- people who saw the website and called us
- someone who connected with us on social media
- someone we met at a tradeshow or convention

This type of prospecting always yields the best results. Sending out printed material or digital-type initiatives like email campaigns, then following up on leads produced by campaigns, is also a great source. This too is a warm call because the potential new client is already interested, or they would not have reached out. There are many others in between "cold" and "warm" here, but the idea is to expose potential clients to the value that you can bring. The thing to remember is to never "sell." Listen intently, then suggest solutions. Being a trusted advisor, not a seller, is the key.

The other end of the spectrum and the most hated by all is the *cold call*. It is also the least effective. Most people would rather have their molars pulled out with a pair of pliers than make a cold sales call—especially technical people. That is why it takes a very strong and confident personality to do this task consistently. Typically, these efforts are subject to what I call, "Rule 122."

100 + 20 + 2 = 122

Essentially this means you must make 100 calls to get 20 appointments to yield 2 possible new clients.

This is not something new, and thousands of sales trainers over the years have taught how to best facilitate the cold call method. But the main thing to remember here is that for Rule 122 to happen, a salesperson has to hear, "No, don't call me again" 80 times before he or she hears an, "OK, tell me more." It is not for the faint of heart.

PERSISTENCE AND CONSISTENCY

The most important elements in sales prospecting are persistence and consistency. There are a ton of sales statistics all over the internet that say most salespeople never make more than three attempts, and most buyers buy on the eighth—implying that most sales folks are idiots and missing the boat. That's simply not true, and it is very misleading to the uninformed. Just because something is posted on the internet does not mean the information is correct. Persistence is a virtue of great salespeople, and there is definitely a biblical principle about being persistent (Matthew 7:7). But we should also do so with wisdom. The truth here is, as a salesperson, there is strong merit in not giving up on a potential client too soon. Be persistent, buffered with wisdom and common sense.

One of my favorite sayings is, "sell to no." This means that when the potential client comes to a place where he or she no longer wants you to follow up or reach out anymore, he or she will let you know. Until that point, you need to stay in touch until you get to "no." When you get to "no," stop. But if there is a potential client, and I am convinced that what we offer can solve a problem or resolve a significant pain point, then I will be persistent—not pesky but persistent—until I get to "no."

Remember, there are always three answers in sales:

1. Yes.

2. No.

3. Not right now.

I believe that most "no's" are really "not right now's." If a client is not ready to trust you just yet, or the timing is simply not right, that does not mean "no"; it simply means "not right now." Earning trust takes time. Is it three calls or thirty? Should I call, send an email, send a hand-written note, or share something of technical interest I found on the internet? Yes, to all. That depends on the client and the situation. If you continue to show interest in the client and their problems and you are persistent without being pesky, you will eventually get to that place where the client is ready to buy or you are certain the opportunity is dead.

The second key point here is consistency. It has been said many times that sales is a lot like bass fishing. It's not so much about skill as it is about how many casts you make.

Simple but true. How often should a salesperson reach out to a potential client? Weekly? Monthly? Quarterly? This is a very subjective area. There is no hard and fast rule. Understanding the urgency and really listening to the potential client is always the best barometer.

 Establish upfront what you _feel_ is best for frequency of contact, then be consistent. If you decide to call weekly, then call weekly. This will demonstrate your commitment to earning trust.

If you are not sure, just ask, "Is it OK if I check back every week?" Most folks will tell you if you listen. If a client tells you to check back in three weeks, then put three weeks on your calendar. Don't call them every week! If they finally tell you there is no need to call back, then stop. Common sense and respect are staples in this endeavor. Use your head, and treat potential clients as you would want to be treated. Move on to the next potential, and archive them for a future "yes."

IDENTIFYING PAIN POINTS

The term _pain points_ has been mentioned a few times, and it may need a bit of clarification. A "pain point" is a specific problem that prospective customers are experiencing. Think of pain points as problems, plain and simple. Customer pain points vary greatly, depending on the unique issues of the client. Most clients are really not aware of these business pain points. Our job is to bring them out and offer solutions. It sounds harsh to say we need to sell to a client's pain points. When you say it out loud, it may conjure up images of the funeral parlor guy calling the grieving widow, trying to upsell her husband's casket from pine to titanium because that's what her husband would have wanted. Really?

The truth is, what we in the sales world define as pain points are not the same kind of pain as in the previous example. There are many kinds of pain. The pain we are talking about here is the pain someone feels when they cannot get something accomplished because (1) they do not know what to do, (2) they do not have the time or the money, or (3) their team is so engaged with other more important things that it's simply a matter of resource limitations. As we have said,

 The mission of any business development team is to build a devoted and trustworthy client base. One of the best and strongest ways to do that is to help our clients resolve their pain.

Doing this is a two-step process:

1. Identify the pain
2. Provide a solution

Some time back, there was a medium-sized city in the Southeast U.S. that our firm had been trying for years to win over as a client. My predecessors had sent a variety of marketing collateral pieces and numerous proposal responses over the years but never seemed to get any opportunity or even get shortlisted as a potential vendor partner on any projects. One day I asked our business developer for that region to just pick up the phone and reach out to the city engineering director and ask if we could buy him and his team lunch. Everybody's got to eat lunch, right? So what would the harm be?

The director agreed, so he and his senior project engineer met me and my business developer downtown for a very pleasant meal. During that lunch meeting we learned that, in the past year, they had awarded numerous contracts to other firms. We also discovered that the director had assigned the senior project engineer responsibility over the selection committee for the city projects we had submitted on. When we asked if he was familiar with our firm, he said he thought he remembered seeing some of our materials and responses to his RFQs (request for qualifications submittals) but didn't really know much about our firm. That was code, by the way, for *our proposal never made it to committee.* He also told us that since there were several more local companies they were comfortable using, they never had really considered us an option anyway.

This was not very promising. But I took a breath, and I asked them both my favorite pain point question: "I know there are a lot of issues you both are concerned about, but if you had to choose one issue or project that keeps you up at night, what would that be?"

The director pondered for a moment, then spoke up. "The 4th Street bridge over Buckley's Creek! It's a main artery inside the city and is in very poor repair. Since it's not a state or federal road, the bridge belongs to the city, and money to rebuild the bridge would have to come from our general fund. The problem is, we don't have the money in our budget to fix it this year, and I really worry about public safety."

OK then—we had identified his primary pain point: step one. Sometimes all you need to do is just ask and listen. But our best chance at becoming a valued resource is for us to move to step two in the process: provide a solution.

It just so happened that our firm was an expert in transportation structures and bridge design, but even better was that the business developer with us at the table was also

93

our grant administration specialist. So I asked the director, "If we could assist you in getting an 80/20 state grant to rebuild that bridge, where you only had to fund twenty cents on the dollar, would that help?"

The director responded, "I would put you on my Christmas list."

So we assisted the city administrator in writing a grant for the bridge using advanced innovative design (AID). The city secured the grant and was able to put the design and construction out for competitive bid. The project was underway in about six months.

Our firm made a small investment helping them secure the grant, but we solved the director's primary pain point and built client loyalty. The firm is now a trusted resource to that city.

 Understanding their needs instead of conveying our wants creates an environment of trust, sharing, and mutual respect that translates into future business.

It's also a win-win for everyone. Remember the real estate agent example: "If I can help you get what you need, I will get what I want"? This is a staple in the arsenal of the sales pillar of business development.

5.

CUSTOMER SERVICE

Customer service and ensuring the best customer experience possible is the next great frontier of business development.

I f you ask a dozen people on the street what makes up business development, the most obvious answer would be "sales" and "marketing." This is a perfectly normal response and how most companies look at and organize themselves. But as we just discussed, there are three pillars or "legs" of this trilogy of business development stool, and each is equally important to its overall stability.

But if you were to force me to choose the one that has the biggest impact on the overall health of any business development engine, it would have to be customer service. Not customer service as a stand-alone department in some call center, answering calls and complaints, but customer service as a function of interacting and nurturing relationships with existing clients. Customer service today is perceived as a place where customers complain, and companies explain to them they have no reason to complain. Customer service is a catch-all for a host of things and is even referred to by many different names: customer success, customer care, client services engagement, and client relations are just a few, and we will go into much more detail on these later.

For purposes of this discussion, think of customer service in terms of how you maintain the relationship with existing clients. In many organizations there is an account rep or client rep that leads this role and serves as emissary or liaison, combining sales and customer service functions specifically to support existing clients.

PARETO'S PRINCIPLE

With all this in mind, if you take an honest look at your overall revenue creation picture, there is a sobering fact that emerges.

 If you apply Pareto's principle to the trilogy, you quickly realize that 80 percent of your business's revenue comes from existing clients; therefore, it is the most important segment of your engine.

What do I mean by Pareto's principle?

The Pareto principle is very simple, yet very important. It is named after Italian economist Vilfredo Pareto, who, legend has it, found that 80 percent of the peas in his garden came from just 20 percent of the plants. Pareto later discovered and proved, using this same observational principle, that 80 percent of the land in Italy was controlled by only 20 percent of the population. Since those revelations, we have come to realize that this 80/20 rule applies to just about anything we analyze (hence, "Pareto's principle"). It has proven especially true for me as I have watched and engaged the business development process in a variety of different venues and companies. Regardless of the product or service we were promoting, the 80/20 rule always seemed to prevail as a constant.[19]

This thought process produces a profound observation regarding your existing customer base. According to Smallbiztrends.com, 80 percent of your company's future profit will come from just 20 percent of your existing customers.[20] I have observed that the revenue statistics are very similar. Given these rough percentages, one can quickly see the impact that a sales + customer service interaction has on success and how truly important it is to your business development engine.

So if 80 percent of your revenue comes from existing customers, and 80 percent of that portion comes from only 20 percent of your client base, then that means if you are a $50MM small B2B business with one thousand steady clients, then hypothetically,

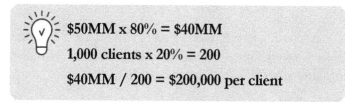

$50MM x 80% = $40MM

1,000 clients x 20% = 200

$40MM / 200 = $200,000 per client

This shows us that the health of your company is in the hands of only two hundred people! Of course, the numbers vary from company to company, and if you are a start-up company or a newly formed division within an existing one, it will be much less. But when these new groups do reach cruising altitude, they will find this will be true for them as well.

19. Kevin Kruse, "The 80/20 Rule and How It Can Change Your Life," *Forbes.com*, 2016. Retrieved from https://www.forbes.com/sites/kevinkruse/2016/03/07/80-20-rule/#773eafa63814.

20. Matt Mansfield, "Customer Retention Statistics—The Ultimate Collection for Small Business," *Small Business Trends*, 2018. Retrieved from smallbiztrends.com/2016/10/customer-retention-statistics.html.

The takeaway here is that no matter how you spin it, customer service is not only a critical element of any business development engine, but it very well could be the most important piece of the pie.

In my thirty years of working in the B2B arena, I have personally observed that in an established company, the actual numbers are more like 75 percent of gross annual sales from existing clients and 25 percent from newly acquired ones. Exact statistical numbers are not as important here as the idea, so don't get hung up on whether it is 72.9 or 81.6 in your situation.

In the world of non-profits, I have also been told that very similar ratios apply to recurring donation revenue. This balance historically seems to provide for the most robust on-going revenue picture with the least risk. We said we think of business development as the "engine" that keeps your company healthy and alive. The existing client base is the lifeblood of that engine and should be nurtured and cared for accordingly.

According to published statistics by Bain and Co., "a 5% increase in customer retention can increase a company's profitability by 75%."[21] That means that,

 If we give as much of our business development energy to customer service as we do to sales and marketing, the impact to the bottom line will be more immediate and less expensive than any other technique.

---

21. Alex Lawrence, "Five Customer Retention Tips for Entrepreneurs," *Forbes.com*, 2012. Retrieved from www.forbes.com/sites/alexlawrence/2012/11/01/five-customer-retention-tips-for-entrepreneurs/#37dd15d15e8d.

CUSTOMER SERVICE IS ABOUT PEOPLE

In the early 1980s I had the good fortune to be a part of the phenomenon known as Federal Express. Through an obvious act of divine providence, I was invited to join the early ranks and be exposed to a culture and an ideal that would influence my life, my management style, and my career forever. Frederick W. Smith, the founder of FedEx, ingrained in all of us a very simple philosophy:

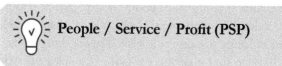 **People / Service / Profit (PSP)**

Get the best and most passionate *people* you can find, treat them like you would want to be treated, and give them the tools and resources they need to succeed. They in turn will take care of the *service,* and the *profit* will take care of itself!

Mr. Smith clearly understood that to develop and maintain a loyal and devoted customer base, he had to empower his greatest assets (his employees) with the ability to deliver his message of value, ensure never-before-seen products and services were delivered as promised, and assure that the customer's service experience was nothing short of astounding. And the rest, as they say, is history.

J. W. Marriott is often quoted as saying, "If you take care of your people, your people will take care of your customers, and your business will take care of itself." Mr. Smith and FedEx are a living example of this philosophy.

The thing that has always baffled me is that most sales and marketing folks rarely consider this People / Service / Profit idea as the single biggest initiative of the company sales engine, if they consider it part of the combined initiative at all. Ken Blanchard is the author of one of the most famous and established business books of all time: *The One Minute*

Manager.[22] One of the primary messages in that book is that customer service is the responsibility of the entire company, not just one department. I could not agree with him more.

Just as we discussed earlier and will explore again throughout this text, with today's silos and segmented thinking, it is very easy to see why most organizations have historically thought of customer service as an operational issue and not one of sales. I have heard many sales folks say, "The customer service department is charged with solving issues and keeping our clients happy." Their thought is that once sales has developed a client, the responsibility for retention belongs to someone else. This is dangerous. If you do not believe that customer service is a sales initiative, consider the following.

In 1990 United Airlines aired a TV commercial entitled, "Speech." The piece was a marketing tool to sell seats on airplanes, but the content makes an enormous statement about customer service. The actors portray a corporate business development setting (sales meeting) where the obvious company leader tells the group of a devastating issue that has just come to his attention. I can't recall the exact wording, but it can be paraphrased like this:

> This morning I got a call from a client we have had for twenty years. He fired us! Told me he doesn't know us anymore. I think I know why. We used to do business with a handshake. Now it's a phone call or a fax. Followed up by another fax. Something's gotta change.

Fax? In 1990 that was high technology. With all the digital tools today like email, Facebook, LinkedIn, texts, and Twitter, we find ourselves (and our kids, especially) losing our ability to look someone in the eye and speak one on one.

---

22. Ken Blanchard, *The One Minute Manager* (NY: William Morrow Publishing, 1982).

The simple truth is that you cannot maintain a relationship with just technology. Customer service needs to embrace any and all of the latest technology available when it enhances the customer experience, but nothing will ever replace human-to-human contact!

At our firm we have a receptionist and operator that is truly amazing. April answers every call with the same delightful, courteous attitude and provides a level of consistent customer service that is off the charts. I try and thank her periodically—but not nearly enough. She may be the most important member of our customer service team.

When a potential or existing client calls or comes by, April represents the very first impression of the firm many clients get. When someone calls angry, in a panic, or with some sort of pain point, she always listens to them, evaluates the situation, and ensures that person gets immediate attention and is funneled to the right place. The value of her attitude is immeasurable.

We have had numerous clients over the years take the time to call and share how wonderful April made them feel; but for every one that calls, I imagine there are a thousand that don't. Imagine the damage and the potential for lost clients that could result if she was curt or rude. You would never know until it was too late. Customer service is about people, and April's example is the basis of the customer service pillar.

HOLD ON A MINUTE

Have you ever called the customer service line to ask a simple question about your bill, and forty-five minutes later you are still on hold, listening to a collection of love songs from the 1980s?

Have you ever called into your local cable provider to find out why the screen went blank during the big game? After ten minutes of negotiating a maze of selections to press on your keypad (none of which seem to apply to your issue), you find yourself listening to the little voice that says the average wait time is an hour. Or, "Your call is important to us . . . so please enjoy this forty-minute flute solo!" Then, after waiting, you finally get someone in Thailand, and English is not their primary language?

Have you ever hired a home repair company to come figure out what's wrong with your heater because it's twelve degrees outside and inside feels like the tundra? They tell you someone will be there between noon and 5 p.m. tomorrow. You take your valuable vacation time from work and wait patiently, only to be called at 6 p.m. by the technician, explaining that he ran into some trouble and it will have to be rescheduled for next week?

Of course you have experienced at least one of these things. We all have. How many new client referrals do you think you will provide to any of those companies? You likely can't wait to leap onto Facebook or Twitter and share your frustration with a few hundred thousand people.

 No amount of marketing dollars or website hits or advertising campaigns will EVER reproduce the power of a loyal customer spreading his or her positive experience about your company.

TRENDING TOWARDS TOTAL CUSTOMER

In 2017 Salesforce.com produced an annual "State of Sales" report designed to provide an overview of the sales industry and map out the trends and sales statistics that underscore just how much approaches and attitudes toward sales are changing. It was very in-depth and listed several trends in sales. The following is a paraphrased excerpt of just two of the topics that were very relevant. The two trends that caught my eye and directly apply to the trilogy philosophy are as follows:

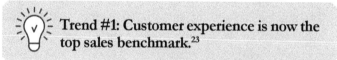

Trend #1: Customer experience is now the top sales benchmark.[23]

Fifty-one percent of sales leaders are focused on increasing customer retention through deeper relationships. They are nearly as focused on customer retention as sales prospecting (56 percent focused on growing leads/new customers). Top sales teams care just as much about creating long-lasting customers through memorable experiences as they do about making the sale.

High-performing sales teams are 2.8 times more likely than underperforming teams to say their sales organizations have become much more focused on personalizing customer interactions over the past twelve–eighteen months.

Seventy-nine percent of business buyers say it's absolutely critical or very important to interact with a salesperson who is a trusted advisor—not just a sales rep—who adds value to their business.

---

23. Tiffany Bova, "26 Sales Statistics that Prove Sales Is Changing," *Salesforce.com*, 2019. Retrieved from https://www.salesforce.com/blog/2017/11/15-sales-statistics.html.

The top two process challenges that sales organizations face are meeting customer expectations and dealing with competitive concerns.

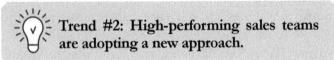

Trend #2: High-performing sales teams are adopting a new approach.

Seventy-three percent of sales teams say collaborating across departments is absolutely critical or very important to their overall sales process. Sales teams of all performance levels realize the importance of cross-collaboration in order to have complete visibility into the customer journey. Sales organizations can no longer exist in silos—they must now connect across different departments, channels, and partners.

Sixty percent of sales professionals say that collaborative selling has increased productivity by more than 25 percent, and more than half (52 percent) say it has done the same for increasing pipeline.

Sixty-eight percent of sales professionals say it is absolutely critical or very important to have a single view of the customer across departments/roles. Yet only 17 percent of sales teams rate their single view of the customer capabilities as outstanding.

Customer service and cross-selling/collaboration are the top two trend movements today. That means that a lot of companies are already either embracing or moving towards the trilogy concept. The vast majority are going to have to catch up.

The last paragraph of trend #2 is most intriguing: "single view of the customer." What do they mean by this? A single customer view is an overall, holistic representation of the information about a single customer that can be viewed in one place by everyone on the business development team. That means that a client is *not* a client of a single department or region but a client of the entire company! Let's add to that—when a client looks at your company or talks with anyone representing your company, they also get a holistic view of what you do and what you can do to help solve their problems.

I worked in a company where the firm had fourteen or fifteen different departments or silos, each providing a different service. One day I did a ride-along call with one of the department heads, visiting a long-term client of the firm. We were sitting in the client's office, talking about his current project, and he told us that things were going well, and our staff was doing a terrific job. (Hard not to grin when a client says that, I know. Feels great!) As we talked and I began to drill down, looking for any possible pain points, he mentioned that he really needed to find someone that could perform a specific environmental evaluation of a section of the project. Since this guy had been a client of ours for twenty-plus years, I was a little taken aback that he didn't know we had a complete department that was filled with experts in that specific field! When I told him about our extensive skill set in that arena, he looked at me and said the seven words of death: "I didn't know you guys did that!"

Each department within the firm acted like an independent company and rarely shared client info or made an effort to cross-sell other services to *their* clients. This does not mean that each of the departments were evil or were trying to undermine their sister groups, but what it does mean is that, as leaders, we did not foster a culture of cross pollination.

Consider if you were to gather all the folks in your company into a big circle and ask each one of them, "What business are you in?" Each one would answer something like, "I'm in the accounting business," or "I'm in the engineering business," or "I work in the equipment service business," or "I am in warehousing and logistics." But the entire group would be wrong. Say the name of your company is AJAX Construction. Every single person at your company is in the construction business! Each simply works in a different construction support group.

It's all about perception. It's all about the culture and climate that leadership creates. What would your folks say?

INDIFFERENCE IS DEATH

As I pointed out in the introduction, the power of customer service and the principles we are discussing are not indicative of our modern world. Currently there is a 3,800-year-old Babylonian tablet in the British Museum in London that appears to be from ancient Mesopotamia and may be the oldest documented customer complaint known to man. The message was written around 1750 B.C. This clay tablet is a written customer service complaint regarding how a man was delivered the wrong grade of copper ore. Here is a paraphrased transcription of generally what the tablet says:

> When you came, you said to me as follows: "I will give Gimil-Sin (when he comes) fine quality copper ingots." You left then but *you did not do what you promised me.* You put ingots which were not good before my messenger (Sit-Sin) and said: "If you want to take them, take them; if you do not want to take them, go away!"

> What do you take me for, that you treat somebody like me with such contempt? I have sent as messengers' gentlemen like ourselves to collect the bag with my money (deposited with you) but you have treated me with contempt by sending them back to me empty-handed several times, and that through enemy territory. Is there

anyone among the merchants who trade with Telmun who has treated me in this way? You alone treat my messenger with contempt!

On account of that one (trifling) mina of silver which I owe(?) you, you feel free to speak in such a way, while I have given to the palace on your behalf 1,080 pounds of copper, and umi-abum has likewise given 1,080 pounds of copper, apart from what we both have had written on a sealed tablet to be kept in the temple of Samas. How have you treated me for that copper? You have withheld my money bag from me in enemy territory; it is now up to you to restore (my money) to me in full. Take cognizance that (from now on) I will not accept here any copper from you that is not of fine quality. I shall (from now on) select and take the ingots individually in my own yard, *and I shall exercise against you my right of rejection because you have treated me with contempt.*[24]

As you can see in the emphasized portions of the paraphrase, an angry customer is a lost customer—and that has not changed much in almost four thousand years! I would wager that he went out of his way to tell all his friends and neighbors far and wide to get their copper from anyone but this merchant.

So, what's the big deal? Sure, a few customers will not be happy; but to make an omelet, "Ya gotta break a few eggs," right? If you do a little internet surfing on customer relations and the problem of poor customer service, you will find a host of people talking about the impact of this very subject on the future of business right now.

24. Liz Leafloor, "4,000-Year-Old Ancient Babylonian Tablet Is Oldest Customer Service Complaint Ever Discovered," *Ancient Origins*, 2015. Retrieved from www.ancient-origins.net/artifacts-ancient-writings/4000-year-old-ancient-babylonian-tablet-oldest-complaint-020313.

WHY DO WE LOSE CUSTOMERS?

Recently there have been several studies that indicate approximately 70 percent of customers that leave a company or business relationship do so because they have perceived or been shown an attitude of indifference by the company. Seventy percent? *Indifference?* What exactly does that mean?

Depending on what dictionary you look at, you get a variety of answers. But for the most part, *indifference* means a lack of interest or concern. It appears that some companies simply don't care about customers. I know, crazy, huh? Perception, as we all know, is everything.

 Even if your employees aren't really being that indifferent, if clients feel or think they are, it can kill your business, and you may never even know it.

PERCEPTION AND DELIVERY OF PROMISE

 Regardless of what is real or perceived, the customer's perception is your reality.

As we analyze both marketing and sales, we find that although there are certainly deliverables involved, the bulk of the first two pillars (marketing/sales) is about *talk* and *promises*. Both of these pillars are paramount to the trilogy, but the true test for any business development engine is in the delivery of those promises (customer service). The first time a client agrees to use your company or buy your product is important, very important, but not nearly as important as the second time. If their perception is that you made good on the marketing and sales promises, then we are on our way to building client loyalty.

All issues are relative in terms of importance or seriousness in the grand scheme of things, *but my problems are important to me*. People want to feel that if they reach out with an issue, someone at your company really cares about their problem and is going to help.

Some companies have mounted campaigns to combat the issue of people not feeling genuinely cared about. In 2016 one small manufacturer of commercial products implemented a program to have members of the senior leadership team call clients and ask three basic questions:

1. Did you receive the products you purchased?

2. Do you have any concerns or questions?

3. Is everything OK, and are you satisfied?

Personal touch is always the best approach, but I realize it is also not always practice. This technique works great for small businesses, but the larger the company gets the more difficult it will be. However, since it isn't possible for such a personal touch in larger companies, some (like AutoZone) use follow-up contests on their receipts. Customers are instructed to go to a certain website and enter to win a prize after they tell the company about their experience. Lowe's, Home Depot, and Kroger all do similar things—excellent campaigns with the prime objective of getting feedback and giving the client a voice.

Netflix did not kill the cable industry; ridiculous fees and horrible service did. Uber did not wound the taxi business; limited taxi access and fare control did. Apple did not stifle the music industry; being forced to buy full-length albums did. Easier service and a better customer experience triumphed in each case. The message here is quite simple:

 Not focusing on existing client happiness is one of the biggest mistakes for any business. The future of any organization depends on their happiness.

The most important thing to remember so far about customer service as it applies to the trilogy is not to think of this pillar as a department you may have in place or a preconceived idea that customer service equals an eight hundred number, website, or online chat person. Those tactical elements of customer service are pieces of the whole, indeed, and crucial to the overall success of the company. But these are tactics—not strategy.

Think of customer service as a strategic concept. Remember, the concept of nurturing and retaining the existing client base and creating long-term, true client loyalty is the holy grail of business development.

We have said that all three pillars of the trilogy are equal. But when it comes to stability and staying power, they are really not. Customer service may actually be more important than selling to new clients, and customer service marketing is just as important as marketing to new clients. Making customer service the flagship of the business development fleet will secure and expand the existing client revenue base. This must be priority one. Focusing ample energy on customer service will provide the financial strength and company security for sales and marketing to then carry the message far and wide to new clients, growing both revenue and profits for the company long term.

6.

LEADERSHIP AND VISION

People do not quit companies, they quit managers.

Leadership. Not supervision or management, but leadership—servant leadership. We will talk more about the role of sound management later in the book, but leadership is an entirely different thing.

If there was going to be a fourth leg or essential element of the business development stool analogy, it would have to be leadership. Every powerful business development team that has been successful has had a great coach—someone with strong leadership skills. And without a doubt, the essential element to such great leadership is humility. Without a measure of it, no leader will ever rise to greatness or develop his or her business development team to its full potential.

 An essential element of any business development strategy is ensuring that the right leader is in the front seat of the business development bus.

There are literally thousands of great books on leadership, and to learn more about what being a "real" servant leader means, look to the works of some of the truly inspirational and spiritual leadership teachers such as John Maxwell, Patrick Lencioni, Zig Ziglar, Jim Collins, and Tony Dungy—to name a few.

No business development would ever happen without people, as has been pointed out already several times. Without question, the greatest asset in any company is its people. People buy from people. Your people. But for business development people to be effective and truly reach the level of success and growth desired from any team, true visionary servant leadership is required. Humility is its core, but true servant leaders also require courage, vision, integrity, and something that I call *diplomatic grit*. Diplomatic grit is knowing when to be firm but fair. Being able to mentor through guidance without the need for power or intimidation or control. Having the "grit" to stand up and fight for anyone or anything when the need arises but also knowing when to use force and just how much or how little to apply.

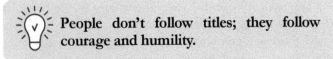 **People don't follow titles; they follow courage and humility.**

For a short period of time I worked at a company in the consumer retail service provider market space. The company was privately held, and there were about four hundred employees. Leadership routinely yelled at and threatened their subordinates. It was the culture from the CEO right down the food chain to the lowly managers.

One day while walking through the hall on the "upper floor" of the corporate building, I heard the CEO yelling at his senior vice presidents in what appeared to be a staff meeting. The atmosphere was "management by fear." Ever been in that sort of work environment or know anyone that has? It is miserable. Nobody thrives; they only exist. Machiavellianism at its finest.[25] *That is not servant leadership.* By the grace of God, I didn't stay there long. That small company did make a profit, but how much more could that team have become if the principles of true servant leadership had been present?

As mentioned earlier, my first exposure to real leadership was at Federal Express. I was a very impressionable young man under the leadership of, in my humble opinion, one of the greatest business leaders of the twentieth century: Mr. Fred Smith. He was and still is a natural leader and most likely the strongest single human influence in my business career. His People / Service / Profit (PSP) philosophy was, at the time, something that I had never witnessed before. The profound impact it had on me and many other emerging leaders has no doubt shaped the future of a great deal of other companies. But even though I thought, at the time, that Mr. Smith had invented this revolutionary concept, I later learned that he was not the first.

The story (as Bill Jr. told it to his daughter in 2015) goes that on a miserably cold and rainy day in 1954, Bill Marriott Sr., the founder of the Marriott hotel chain, invited President Dwight D. Eisenhower to a quail hunt on his farm. The group included Bill Sr., President Eisenhower, a cabinet member, and Bill Sr.'s son, Bill Jr. That morning, being safe and warm in the house, they discussed whether or not to venture out into the wind and cold. At the time, Bill Jr., the youngest in the group, was a twenty-two-year-old Navy ensign.[26] After a few minutes of discussion among the elders, President Eisenhower turned to Bill Jr. and asked, "What do you think?"

---

25. See reference to footnote 12.
26. An ensign is a junior-ranked officer of the armed forces.

Although he was a little dumfounded, Bill Jr. strongly suggested they stay inside where it was warm by the fire. So they did just that. Bill Jr. later said that encounter intrigued him and made an impact on his leadership skills forever. The fact that the most powerful person in the world asked for his opinion demonstrated to him the importance of hearing varied views and gaining consensus.[27] If you think about the impact,

 Eisenhower's simple question could be the four most important words in leadership: "What do you think?"

Good leaders practice this every single day.

This story of President Eisenhower and Bill Marriott Jr. has been told hundreds of times I am sure, and you may have already heard it or read a similar account—but it's still worth repeating. If we stop and think about it for a moment, this simple question really embodies three foundations of exceptional leadership:

1. Break the leadership bubble.

2. Demonstrate true humility.

3. View others as equals.

ARE LEADERS BORN OR TRAINED?

Everyone has the opportunity to be a leader in some capacity at some point in his or her life. I am certain that, like salespeople, some people have the DNA to be great leaders from birth—and some do not. But even if you are not a born leader, I believe that the traits of a good leader can be

27. Ethan Rothstein, "What Eisenhower Taught Bill Marriott about Leadership," *Bisnow.com*, 2015. Retrieved from https://www.bisnow.com/washington-dc/news/hotel/bill-marriott-on-leadership-millennials-and-eisenhower-51300.

learned with patience and practice. The authors mentioned in the introduction are a terrific place to start, as is following the biblical principles of the greatest New Testament servant leader known to man, Jesus. But if a person *has* the desire, they can in fact become a good leader.

Thomas Jefferson was without question one of the greatest leaders we have ever known. He was not only the author of the Declaration of Independence, the third president of the United States, the secretary of state, the ambassador to France, and the founder of the University of Virginia, but he was an extraordinary man that was not a born leader. By his own admission! Throughout his life, he aspired to become and grow into a great leader by being willing to learn how to lead through change, humility, and patience. In his writings on leadership, Jefferson outlined many ideas and key points that echo this attitude. Here is a paraphrase of eight that I have remembered over the years:

1. Leadership is not about you, but about the people you serve.

2. Be honest and do what is right.

3. Do not gather authority, but seek to share and distribute it.

4. Be wise and self-limiting in the exercise of authority.

5. Do good work with a humble spirit and a low profile.

6. Change comes slowly, but it comes inevitably.

7. Expect opposition.

8. Know when to stop leading and pass the baton.

You don't have to be Thomas Jefferson to be a good leader. A person can learn to be a leader if they are teachable and humble.

Remember, mediocre leaders *push*, good leaders *explain*. Even better leaders *show*, but the really great leaders *inspire*.

One of my favorite business leaders is Richard Branson. Being a bit of a rebel myself, I think my fascination with him is due to his unique approach to traditional paradigms. His Virgin empire[28] did not happen overnight and had more failures than successes, according to his personal account.

One of the things that really stuck with me was his answer to the question, *What do you look for in leaders?* In a 2017 INC.com article, Sir Richard addressed this commonly asked question.[29] He said that what he values most is leaders that show genuine interest and care for their people. People don't come to work simply for the money; they want to be a part of the team, be listened to, and be appreciated. Sort of sums it all up, huh?

Another compelling author is Tony Dungy. In his book *The Mentor Leader* he outlines what he refers to as *mentor leadership*. Growing, mentoring, and nurturing people to develop strong character, integrity, meaningful relationships, and eternal values.[30] It's strong stuff.

If you stand back and look at what all these great leaders share, it is the recurring theme of Mr. Smith's People / Service / Profit (PSP) philosophy. Surround

---

28. "Richard Branson is an entrepreneur and businessman, who founded the Virgin group of more than 400 companies. The Virgin group grew from a small record shop he founded in 1972, to become a major multinational company including interests in transport, media, and entertainment." Tejvan Pettinger, "Biography of Richard Branson," Oxford, www.biographyonline.net, 5th Feb. 2013. Last updated 1 February 2018. Retrieved from https://www.biographyonline.net/business/richard_branson.html.

29. John Eades, "Richard Branson Knows What to Look for in Leaders: Here's What It Is," *Inc.com*, 2017. Retrieved from https://www.inc.com/john-eades/richard-branson-knows-what-to-look-for-in-leaders-heres-what-it-is.html.

30. Tony Dungy, *The Mentor Leader* (Carol Stream, IL: Tyndale House, 2010).

yourself with great people and give them the tools they need to create ecstatic clients. They will, in turn, take care of the service, and the profit will take care of itself. How much simpler can it be?

The trilogy concept uses the stool analogy to demonstrate the three critical synergies of the over-arching philosophy of business development and how interdependent each is on the other. The point of our leadership discussion is that,

 Any business development organization, whether it is as complex as Google or a small, twenty-person accounting firm with a single office, *must* have a coach or captain to lead the team to victory. Someone with vision, courage, passion, humility, strength, *diplomatic grit*, and servant leadership, capable of understanding all the moving parts and able to empower the people to create and sustain client loyalty.

Everything rises and falls on great leadership. Without great leadership, the very best business development strategy is doomed to fail. Dan Cathy is one of my all-time favorites:

> Successful leaders view the journey more like the captain of a sailboat, relying on their skill and know-how, but knowing all along that the wind [help from other sources] is the force that will get them to their destination.[31]

---

31. Quote by Dan Cathy, CEO of Chick-fil-A. Referenced in Brian Dodd, "15 Leadership Quotes from Dan Cathy, Chick-fil-A President and COO," *Churchleaders.com*, 2011. Retrieved from https://churchleaders.com/pastors/pastor-blogs/151559-brian_dodd_15_leadership_quotes_from_dan_cathy_chick-fil-a_president.html.

7.

SUPPORTING ROLES

S o far, the marketing, sales, and customer service team
members outlined have been employees that interact
directly with clients. But on any business development team,
there are two distinct types of staff:

1. Customer-facing

2. Supporting

The first is obvious. Customer-facing roles for any
BD team would be people as previously described: front-
line sales reps, account managers, business developers,
marketing campaign managers, and customer service agents.
However, there is also a wide variety of supporting duties
and functions that are just as important. Some of the roles
are new, but most of them have been around for decades and
serve valuable time-tested functions. These include people
like,

- advertising specialists
- marketing consultants
- interns of all sorts
- public relations specialists

- lead generation staff
- artwork and design creatives
- leadership roles
- clericals and administrative
- training staff
- human resources
- research analysts
- data specialists
- webmasters

Some have partial customer-facing duties, but for the most part, these key players provide the critical support and backup functions *mandatory* for the success of any business development engine.

Most of us are familiar with these and have a good understanding of what they do and the value each can add, so there is no need for me to explain or to go into intimate detail about each. The important thing to remember is that these team members are part of the business development engine just as much as the front-line sales staff. The essential challenge for the business development leadership team is empowering them *all* to feel a part of the whole.

Even though most of these positions listed are well established, some roles are quite new and have not been around long enough for us to really judge their value. Early on we discussed how complicated we have made business development, with silos and segregated departments that do a poor job of sharing information and embracing the idea of a *single customer view*. Because of this, some new functions, jobs, and even entire departments have been created to try and solve problems and improve the customer experience. Some were born from pure need because of the evolution of the sales process due to technology and the change in the sophistication level of B2B buyers. Others are a result of the complicated, segregated, and competing organizations we ourselves have created.

With all this in mind, let's talk about a few of these newer functions/jobs/departments that are relevant to the conversation.

SALES ENABLEMENT

Sales enablement is a relatively new term and describes an employee that serves as liaison between sales and marketing. By various definitions, sales enablement is chartered with ensuring that sales staff have the relevant, client-specific, and compelling sales tools and resources they need to be more effective and efficient. Brochures, presentations, client relationship management information (customer relationship management, or CRM—there is a description of what this tool is in Step 7), digital tools and applications, best sales practice training, and scorekeeping metrics are just a few of the deliverables of any sales enablement function. Some recent published data cites that roughly . . .

- 60 percent of B2B buyers feel that sales content is not specific to their needs.
- 64 percent of B2B decision makers say they won't engage a salesperson if the communication is not more personalized.
- 67 percent of all salespeople do not meet their goals.[32]

The thought process here is that traditional sales material and methods may not be giving clients the level of sophistication, data, and specifics that they want. Sales enablement was created to assist sales staff in the development

---

32. These data are hybrids of various sources.

and delivery of more client-specific and content-driven information.

 This new role appears to provide a combination of services historically performed by marketing, sales support, and sales training, individually packaged into a neat bundle.

Bringing these tasks into a single job description in order to better serve the client is not really a bad idea. After all, ensuring that the people who deliver the message of value to new and existing clients have the best tools and support possible is crucial.

Think about a pro golfer. He or she has a ton of natural talent, but with better clubs or the latest course ranging technology, they can be even better. That's what sales enablement does for salespeople.

Seeing the B2B industries place so much focus on sales support is very encouraging. The only issue is, where does this function need to reside? Marketing? Sales? Customer service? Many companies have even created an entire new group called, "sales enablement." Embrace the idea because it is very sound. But before an entire new department emerges, evaluate your organization and determine specifically what is best for you.

CUSTOMER EXPERIENCE

The customer experience function is responsible for the overall customer impression of the company, using every customer interaction as an opportunity to build a better customer experience. These folks should be a part of the customer service pillar, fluidly interacting with the other two pillars. They are responsible for the strategy, design, and execution of ways and ideas to improve how the company interacts with clients.

Customer experience is chartered with leading and inspiring change and innovation in spite of existing culture, processes, and incentives. This group will bring expertise in building, leading, and motivating service-focused teams and implementing best practices driven towards enhancing the customer experience. This should be the place where client feedback and conversations are assembled and acted upon. Appointing someone to own the customer experience is a terrific idea. Most successful, larger B2B companies embrace it and use this function to innovate and improve on a continual basis.

CLIENT ENGAGEMENT

The customer engagement specialist or client engagement manager role can be confusing. Some companies utilize these people as basically sales or account representatives—serving the same function of engaging new and existing clients. Others in service-related industries use client engagement managers to interact with clients regarding collections and billing issues, invoicing, general accounts receivables, and contract management. After some research, I was able to find this clarifying job description:

 The customer engagement manager is paid to ensure that clients are engaged with the company's products or services.[33]

33. Allison Tanner, "What Is a Customer Engagement Manager?" *Study. com*, 2018. Retrieved from https://study.com/academy/lesson/what-is-a-customer-engagement-manager.html.

Sounds somewhat ambiguous to me. Hopefully the intent is to foster a better client experience. Quite frankly, this job title appears to be another name for jobs that should be already established. "Sales rep" or "account manager" or "accounts receivable manager" would suffice.

CUSTOMER ADVOCACY

"Customer success manager." "Client advocacy director." These new job titles sound very cool and have emerged over the past few years. Depending upon which job description you read, each has slightly different tasks. The jobs are all different yet seem effectively the same. The mission is to establish and maintain positive client relationships from an operational and strategic perspective—to serve as an advocate or champion of the client.

 By definition, a customer success manager is responsible for developing customer relationships that promote client loyalty.

Customer advocacy is another form of customer service, focused on what is deemed to be best for the customer. The functions and duties of customer advocacy and customer success have always been a part of any great business development effort. Even though the job titles were different or the duties were scattered among various roles, these customer-centric functions have always been present and a very integral part of any successful business development engine.

The truly encouraging part today, however, is that with the advent of all these new job titles, it shows that companies are placing more and more emphasis on customer service.

Ensuring that the existing client is advocated for and new ones are cherished is fundamental to the trilogy concept.

 Given that the financial strength and backbone of any company comes from loyal and happy existing clients, assigning that success to a job function may make perfect sense.

I applaud any company that engages it.

But the only issue that is mildly troubling is the question, *Do we need these unique job functions at all?* Why should our clients need to be advocated for or have someone to ensure their success when they interact with the company? If these functions are a result of companies caring for and nurturing clients to the next level of service excellence, then we should all stand up and cheer them on. This is another great sign of forward momentum and growth.

If, however, this simply supports the reality that we may have created these customer problems ourselves, then there may be a larger issue to consider. In the last few years, a lot of emphasis has been placed on "the customer experience"—which, without a doubt, is the absolute correct approach. As we have pointed out, elated and loyal customers are the primary mission of any company. But I contend that if we have created an environment where the company is the enemy and the customer experience or advocacy person is needed to protect the client from the company, then we must all step back and evaluate why and what we are doing wrong. If our customer experience is that bad, then we need to make some changes. We will address that in Part 2.

The point is that ensuring the customer has a great experience with your company should already be a part of your culture. If your business development team believes in what you do, and if you have empowered all the employees to strive toward client loyalty, you will not need an entire department to advocate for your clients.

Regardless whether a business development member is customer facing or in a support role, part of the marketing, sales, or customer service team segments at the top or bottom of the organizational food chain, each is a link in that wonderful customer experience chain. Each link in the chain must be engaged, caring, strong, and capable. How strong is your chain?

PART 2:

7 STEPS
TO
EVALUATE AND
IMPROVE
THE
BUSINESS
DEVELOPMENT
ENGINE

Goal setting is a total waste of time unless you have a sound plan to make them happen.

PART 2:

7 STEPS

TO

EVALUATE AND
IMPROVE
THE
BUSINESS
DEVELOPMENT
ENGINE

OVERVIEW OF THE 7 STEPS

Seven small steps for you, one giant leap for your business.

Welcome to the action part of the book. Neil Armstrong was a childhood hero of mine. We remember him as an astronaut, adventurer, and fearless pilot. The commander of Apollo 11 and the first man to step foot on the moon. But most forget he was also a designer, an engineer, and a college professor. Both fearless and logical. Strategic and tactical. A rare breed. That is why I chose to pay homage to him with the subtitle of this book. Like Neil, to engage the 7-step process that follows, we must be willing and fearless while at the same time strategic and tactical.

John Maxwell may be my favorite inspirational writer of all time. I absorb all of the books and teachings he produces that I can. His words and ideas on leadership are always succinct, insightful, direct, and deadly accurate. Over the years, his teachings and books have made me think that similar concepts also apply to any good business development plan. So I have boiled it down into these four simple ideas:

1: **Be Innovative and Open Minded**

2: **Encourage Change and Create Improvement Plans**

3: **Then Take Action**

4: **(Rinse and Repeat)**[34]

That's sums up the intent of the next segment of this book. Companies that win do this consistently and passionately.

If all this philosophy and wisdom so far is old news, and you and your business development team are already embracing the trilogy concept, then congratulations! You can stop reading and celebrate that you have a distinct advantage over your competition. However, if not, then you are probably saying, *OK, all this information is grand, and I am convinced that my business development structure needs to evolve . . . but how? What do we do, and how do we proceed?* I am glad you asked.

Before we move forward, it's important to reiterate that the focus of the following seven steps or suggestions in Part 2 of this book is to simply provoke a thought exercise. This stimulated thought can apply to all businesses, regardless of type, geography, size, or product. According to the Census Bureau's Annual Survey of Entrepreneurs in 2016, 99.7 percent of companies in the U.S. have fewer than five hundred employees—99.7 percent! These same small companies employ over half of all Americans and produce 64 percent of all net, new private-sector jobs.[35] My trilogy concept was born from watching these medium-to-small-sized companies struggle with how to grow and build client loyalty. So it stands to reason that of this 99.7 percent, those that are B2B firms and have enough humility to listen will be the ones to reap the most reward from the suggested steps that follow.

---

34. These four ideas were my personal takeaways/notes from one of John Maxwell's talks.

35. "Facts & Data on Small Business and Entrepreneurship," *SBE Council*, 2018. Retrieved from https://sbecouncil.org/about-us/facts-and-data/.

Henry Ford said nothing happens until somebody sells something, right? But the secret he did not share is, who is doing the selling? As I repeatedly mention throughout this entire book,

 The trick to a great business development program is to build an organization of dedicated people that work as a team tirelessly and sincerely for you and your clients.

And we must remember that, as we take a hard look at how we build a client base, growth comes from a variety of places.

The key element that I will continue to reiterate, and most companies fail to embrace, is to empower *all employees* to take ownership in the business development vision, not just the sales folks. Share the vision, strategy, and excitement about whatever you provide with everyone at your company, and in turn they will carry that message to the clients in ways you could not imagine.

Think of business development like a relay race. Each team member has the potential to be just as important as the next. Each has a unique talent, and when placed in the right order, you get the best chance of winning. Begin to think in terms of unity, not separation. Is my current BD team pulling together, sharing information, and structured for success? For those of you that feel that all problems in life boil down to math, then remember the equation of the three pillars:

 $$BD = M + S + CS$$

Regardless of how you visualize it, we have shown that business development is a team sport. We must also encourage everyone on the team to employ the single most important element to success: humility. It's not about us; it's about listening to the client and solving their problems.

Everyone has probably heard the business school example of the drill bit versus the hole. By understanding that the client need is for a hole in the wood and not the purchase of a drill bit, we focus on the outcome or the solution to a client's pain. The client does not necessarily want to buy a drill bit, he only wants a hole in his piece of wood. He wants to buy a hole.

There are many ways to make a hole: you can use a punch and a hammer or a concentrated acid drip, you can buy some termites or even take out the old .44 magnum and blow a hole in it. The mission would be to determine what is important to the client. Does he care about damage to the surrounding wood, or is he just in a super big hurry? Is noise an issue? Is hole size consistency important? The client tells us that speed is not the issue; it is accuracy of hole size and being able to create multiple holes with the same accuracy. Now that we understand his needs, we can offer the drill bit as the right solution. What do your clients really need?

- Disney isn't selling vacations; they sell family memories.

- Harley isn't selling motorcycles; they sell a lifestyle.

- Apple isn't selling gadgets; they sell a digital experience.

So many organizations focus on the features of what they do or sell instead of selling solutions to pain.

 By listening to pain, then providing what the client needs in lieu of what we want him to have, we make a client for life.

We have defined, dissected, and described what business development consists of and how it should be approached. We have talked about the elements and pieces. We have touched on the critical path items and the supporting roles. We have also pointed out that no matter how much technology we may employ, there is no substitute for passionate and committed people. When a team thinks they can win, they do. But like any good puzzle, how do all the parts make a whole? What is the catalyst to stimulate action? Business development in the B2B world boils down to this clarifying statement:

 The mission for any organization is client or customer loyalty. When that is achieved, the company has arrived. By galvanizing all the team members of marketing, branding, public relations, sales, sales support, and customer services, what is created is a client-making machine.

As a result of three decades of winning, failing, and watching others create processes and organizations counterproductive to the core of the trilogy, I have developed seven key steps to assist in evaluating and establishing a business development engine designed to improve client loyalty and ultimately help organizations evolve. The following steps are a basic roadmap to begin the journey of conversion. If your company is a start-up, then these steps can certainly serve as a guide to help establish a BD baseline. But the real value of this plan is for companies that are already in business and not reaching the potential desired or don't have a firm grasp on business development at all. By no means are the steps all-encompassing, but if you use these as a guide for discussion and are rigorously honest and open minded, the result will be eye-opening and produce real improvement.

133

STEP 1:

REVIEW AND EVALUATE

The secret to getting ahead is getting started. (Mark Twain)[36]

S tatistics are everywhere regarding business development failure. Regardless of the actual numbers, the recurring theme is that many more businesses fail than thrive. Why? Even those that seem to be established struggle with healthy business development growth. Interestingly enough, according to published data by Bain and Co., 94 percent of companies with business development problems say that internal issues are the primary barriers to growth, not external challenges.[37] Bureaucracy, segmentation, silos, complex and cumbersome structure, too many meetings, poor communications, as well as the loss of the customer-centric "entrepreneurial" spirit that launched them in the first place, are only a few of the primary reasons cited.

In order to evaluate the current state of our business development engine, we must take a hard look at ourselves.

---

36. https://www.brainyquote.com/authors/mark_twain

37. Ted Bauer, "Business Development: 94% of Challenges Are Internal," *The Context of Things*, 2016. Retrieved from http://thecontextofthings.com/2016/07/23/business-development-challenges/.

As simple as this sounds, most B2B companies, once they are established, rarely step back and honestly self-evaluate. People get busy, processes get established, paradigms evolve, and before we know it, we are in the "rut." The best way to begin this process is to assemble the key stakeholders and thought leaders within your organization (at a quiet place, away from distractions), and attempt to answer these fundamental questions.

WHY ARE WE IN BUSINESS?

This my favorite question. I fell in love with it when I heard it on a live simulcast. If the answer is to just make a profit, then maybe you are in the wrong business. Great companies have a reason to exist, and that reason or vision is shared by the entire company. Define yours as a team and write it down for all to see. Post it in the breakroom, show it on the company intranet, print up some T-shirts, or make stickers for everyone's computer. Talk about it as many times as necessary to ensure that all team members know and feel the vision.

WHAT DO WE SELL, AND WHY?

Let us consider for a moment the Hedgehog Concept. The Hedgehog Concept is based on an ancient Greek parable which said, "The fox knows many things, but the hedgehog knows one big thing." Jim Collins related this metaphor to business in his book, *Good to Great*.[38] This concept describes how companies are divided into two types: foxes and hedgehogs. The fox knows many things. The fox is very cunning, creative, and able to deploy multiple strategies to attack the hedgehog. The hedgehog, on the other hand,

---

38. Jim Collins, *Good to Great: Why Some Companies Make the Leap . . . and Others Don't* (NY: HarperCollins, 2001).

knows one big thing: rolling up into a perfect little ball of sharp spikes. No matter what strategy the fox uses, the hedgehog always wins.[39]

Great business development teams are more like hedgehogs; they know what they do well, and they nurture it. Lesser teams are more like foxes; they pursue many goals and initiatives at the same time, creating business development strategies that are often scattered, confused, and unfocused. They waste time and resources.

Understanding which one you are—fox or hedgehog—is the key. To help discover this, Collins outlined three Hedgehog thought points:

1. What are you deeply passionate about?

2. What are you better at than anyone else in the world?

3. What drives your economic engine?

Another interesting discovery in Collins's book was that strategy did not necessarily separate the great companies from the lesser companies. Both had strategic plans, and there was no evidence that the great companies spent more time on strategic planning than the lesser companies. So what was the secret?

Focus. Focus on what answers these three questions. Focus on what you do best. Developing a strategic business development plan leads to focus for your team members and your customers. We will talk more about developing that plan later, but focus is the key.

If you are a commercial electrical contractor, then you sell one thing: electrical power systems. And hopefully this is your passion. But if you are a commercial office furniture distributor, then you may have thousands of products. Some

---

39. Information on this concept can be found at https://www.mindtools. com/pages/article/hedgehog-concept.htm. "The Hedgehog Concept: Using the Power of Simplicity to Succeed."

of these products are your core staples; some may be slow movers but necessary to augment the core business; and some may not be a good fit for the core business at all. As an office furniture company that is an expert in helping clients choose the best and most cost-effective interior furniture layouts, why in the world did you venture into exterior office lighting? Seemed like a good idea at the time? Didn't really give a lot of strategic, long-range thought to it? One day one of your clients asked if you could install some outdoor lighting and add it to their existing order, and you just did it. Now, five years later, you have a warehouse full of electrical lighting stuff you can't move, and it's killing your inventory budget.

The idea is to focus. Understand what your company sells and in which areas you are the best of the best—subject matter experts.

Maybe there are products you sell or services you have on your list that should not be a part of your offering. Years ago, when I was deeply into Taekwondo, my Master would quote an ancient proverb: "Dog that chase many rabbits never catch any, but dog that chase only one will always catch." Look honestly at each product or service, and be willing to jettison anything that isn't working. Maybe there is a market that is an incredible fit for your team now that has never been considered. Trends change, and market needs change with time. Should you replace office lighting with "ergonomic" workstation design? Clearly understand what you sell, and why.

WHO IS OUR TARGET AUDIENCE?

 Who we are trying to sell to is as important as what we sell.

What does our ideal client look like? Public, private, or non-profit? Domestic or international? Small firms or huge corporations? Trying to be all things to all people is a recipe for disaster. Again, focus is the key to success. Identify the specifics, needs, and demographic of people or businesses that are the best fit for your product or service, then design your strategy and tactical planning around that client target. Be honest, flexible, and keenly aware of what is working and what is not. Then take action.

WHERE ARE WE IN THE MARKETPLACE?

Competition makes the world go around. But understanding your market space and where your company resides on the landscape is paramount to growth.

Several years ago, I was asked to create a business plan for a start-up nutraceutical company. The product was very cool—had a catchy name and was specifically targeted for a small, unique, niche industry. The owners were very passionate about the product and quite excited to borrow money and begin production. But after some basic analysis, we learned that the target market only consisted of about a million or so potential users nationwide. At the price point for this product, even if *every single one of them* purchased the product regularly, the company would barely make a profit.

How big is your market? Who are the key players and competition? How much market share does your company enjoy versus the competition? Do not guess or rely on intuition. If your team does not have the ability to collect this data, I highly suggest paying an outside consultant to help. In this case, knowledge and data give you power.

You should also engage a strategic analysis tool or method like SWOT (Strengths, Weaknesses, Opportunities, Threat), MOST (Mission, Objectives, Strategies, and Tactics), or PEST (Political, Economic, Sociological, and

139

Technological) to evaluate your team and your product to better understand your chance of success.

 Passion and enthusiasm about the product or service are the foundation of any successful company, but don't let them override logic and good judgment.

HOW MUCH DO WE SPEND ON BUSINESS DEVELOPMENT, AND WHERE?

What companies spend on the marketing and sales segments of the trilogy depends on the venue. Highly competitive firms can spend as much as 25 percent of revenue, while smaller companies are fine with 7–8 percent. The average is about 10 percent. That means a B2B firm with gross revenue of $25MM annually should be spending around $2.5MM on sales and marketing. Where that is spent depends upon the strategic and tactical business development plan you create. This plan should have the budget divided into categories that are trackable and make sense for you, with real spending tracked as a variance against the plan. This allows you to specifically understand what you spend and where.

During my career, I have listened to several medium-sized business leaders tell me, "We spend over a million dollars a year on business development. Why are we not thriving?" When I ask how that spending specifically is broken down, they reply that it is simply lumped into a single, *catch-all* category on the general ledger called "business development." This can include a plethora of things like cell phone bills, copy paper, advertising, website maintenance, sales calls, air travel, lunches, spa and club memberships, events, brochures, seminars, conventions, and VP trips to the Bahamas. Sometimes when people are not busy, they just charge time to the "BD" category as a filler to complete their forty hours.

By not specifically categorizing what gets spent on business development, there is no concise way to determine what is working, what is not working, and the return on that investment. Later we will suggest ways to ensure the development of a sound business development plan.

CONCLUSION

"Change management" and "continuous improvement" are two buzz phrases we hear all the time. Why do so many people preach them? Because they are solutions, that's why. Companies grow. As each grows, in many cases the growth just happens without a plan. Departments get created and procedures get developed to solve short-term issues without enough reflection on how it will affect the longer term, and nobody ever revisits those decisions. Products and services get added for the wrong reasons.

Simple, undirected growth is not evolution. Bigger is not always better without a plan. Would you rather have a $35MM company with a 15 percent EBITDA[40] and a 96 percent client retention rate, or a $150MM firm with a 3 percent EBITDA and 40 percent client turnover?

Step back periodically (after one, three, or five years) and take an in-depth look at where you are and where you are going. Start with these basic questions, and feel free to add several of your own. From that review process, if the necessary course corrections are made, then you are *managing the change* or evolution of the business development strategy—it is not managing you.

> *I can't change the direction of the wind, but I can adjust my sails to always reach my destination. (Jimmy Dean)*

---

40. EBITDA refers to earnings before interest, tax, depreciation, and amortization.

STEP 2:

GALVANIZE THE TEAM, AND SEEK CLIENT & EMPLOYEE FEEDBACK

The way a team plays as a whole determines its success. You may have the greatest bunch of individual stars in the world, but if they don't play together, the club won't be worth a dime. (Babe Ruth)[41]

Have you ever driven to the area of town with a lot of fast food places, looking for a place to eat lunch, and all the establishments seem to have a normal crowd except for Chick-fil-A, which is two rows deep and the line is out into the street? Amazing, I know. Have you ever stopped to consider why that is the case?

I believe it is because, instead of trying to lure customers with deals, discounts, and coupons, then get them in and out quickly, Chick-fil-A makes customers feel welcomed—like they matter. Their menu isn't exhaustive, and they offer similar food items to other fast food restaurants, but Chick-fil-A has perfected client loyalty. They are grateful for their

---

41. http://www.baberuth.com/quotes/.

patrons and their employees, and people can feel it when they walk in the door—they truly mean it. They listen to their customers and then adjust accordingly. They are always trying new ways to help their customers get what they want and make their employees feel a part of the family. Chick-fil-A listens. After all, that is why God gave us two ears and one mouth, right?

GALVANIZE THE TEAM

Galvanize. I love that word. It means to stimulate action in others as if done by an electric shock.[42] How do we galvanize our team?

In the mid-twentieth century there was an American engineer, statistician, professor, author, lecturer, and management consultant named Dr. W. Edwards Deming who made an enormous impact on the world with his message of Total Quality Management Principles.[43] He is credited with a Japanese post-war economic miracle when Japan rose from the ashes of WWII and became the second-largest economy in the world—through processes and ideas influenced by Dr. Deming.

In his 1982 book, *Out of the Crisis*,[44] Deming outlined what he felt were the fourteen key points for that success. These points are a set of management practices to help companies increase their quality and productivity. From these principles, I believe the idea of Total Quality Management was born, ultimately leading to what we now call Six Sigma along with a variety of other production improvement methods.

---

42. Merriam-Webster.com, keyword: *galvanize*.

43. Dr. W. Edwards Deming is renowned as the father of quality manufacturing and the Six Sigma programs. "W. Edwards Deming's 14 Points for Total Quality Management," *ASQ, The Global Voice of Quality*, 2019. Retrieved from https://asq.org/quality-resources/total-quality-management/deming-points.

44. W. Edwards Deming, *Out of the Crisis* (Cambridge, MA: MIT Press, 2000).

Although Deming's points are aimed at overall production, there are four underlying ideals that apply directly to our business development discussion. The four applicable ideas roughly translate into the following:

1. Develop and adopt a new philosophy.
2. Adopt and institute leadership.
3. Break down barriers between all staff areas in the company.
4. Put everybody in the company to work, accomplishing the transformation.

Deming's revolutionary suggestions to the Japanese manufacturing community included the idea to involve everyone—from the salespeople to the production floor workers—in the process. They created a "work team" that had a voice and a venue to share their thoughts and potentially better and more efficient ways to do tasks. I learned a long time ago that the best way to sell an idea is to seek comments, input, and ideas from everyone involved.

 This "upfront buy-in," without fail, creates an atmosphere of commitment and resolve among the stakeholders that results in a much higher success rate. The Japanese manufacturing community saw this success.

Zig Ziglar told us for years that just because your business card does not say "sales" does not mean you are not in sales.[45] If you deal with people in any way in your business, you are in sales. To have a vibrant business development engine, the entire company needs to feel they play a part. Create an atmosphere of collaboration—from marketing

---

45. Retrieved from https://www.brainyquote.com/quotes/zig_ziglar_617802.

to quality assurance (QA)/quality control (QC) to the shop floor.

Winning over a new client or being selected for a new project is a win. Everybody likes to win. The mission is to make everyone feel a part of that success, just like Chick-fil-A does. Just because the offensive coordinator for the Dallas Cowboys is not the one that actually carries the ball across the goal line does not mean that he didn't play a crucial role in the team win. One of the greatest football coaches of all time and arguably one of the greatest life coaches as well, Vince Lombardi, once said, "The achievements of an organization are the result of the combined effort of each individual."[46]

Have you ever walked into an office and the reception staff was delightful, helpful, and made you feel welcomed? Offered you some coffee? Remembered your name from your last visit? How did that make you feel? Remember the story of April the receptionist at our firm and how many people commented on her? The positive experience a client has with any employee of the company can be the foundation of trust. When there is a culture of service and a pride of brand that permeates throughout the organization, clients can feel it. When employees feel a part of a winning team and truly believe that, the result is amazing.

Share your business development plan with all the stakeholders in the company, not just managers. Try and make sure everyone in the company knows the plan and mission. Galvanize the team.

PROFIT SHARING AND INCENTIVE

People are all motivated by something. Some folks are motivated by a passion to serve others. Some are driven by

46. Michael Gold, "3 Business Leadership Lessons We Can All Learn from Football," *Intermedia.net,* 2019. Retrieved from https://www.intermedia.net/blog/2019/01/25/3-business-leadership-lessons-we-can-all-learn-from-football/.

a thirst for knowledge or to discover some new scientific breakthrough. There are those that get up every morning with great zeal, searching for a cure for cancer or a new and distant star. These people are incentivized by passion and the quest. I have always admired and envied those kinds of folks. Really admired them. I am grateful to God that there are people like that in our society. Without them, our quality of life would not even be close to what we enjoy today.

The norm in society today is the exchange of hours and energy for dollars.

 We all aspire to be independently wealthy, but in actuality, 94 percent of all Americans work for someone else for pay, with over 75 percent having less than five thousand dollars in savings—doing their best to make as much as they can to take care of their families and their future. And that is perfectly OK.

Profit sharing and incentive plans give employees and non-direct sales folks what we refer to as "skin in the game." If the company makes a profit, they will get to share in that profit. Simple as that. When employees feel they can make a real difference by being frugal with expenses, assisting a team member that is struggling to meet a deadline, or showing clients that their company is truly grateful for their business, they will give it their all. Develop a plan that works for your company. Regardless of the system, it should be fair, consistent, and shared with employees so they feel a part of the growth and know what their reward could be. Offering incentive is not mandatory, but it is a great way to get teams engaged.

147

HOW WELL DO WE KNOW OUR CLIENTS?

How many clients do we have? Who are they? Where are they? Do you know the top 20 percent of your best clients by name? Since 80 percent of the company's revenue comes from 20 percent of your existing client base, should we not know them well? Find out what makes them loyal. If you asked your top ten clients, what would they say they love about your company, product, or service? If you asked the last ten clients that you lost, what would they say? Why not ask them both?

THE EMPLOYEE AND CLIENT LENS

In business, for decades the quest has been for some way to differentiate from the competition. In the 80s it was quality, in the 90s it was brand management, and today it is all about the customer experience . . . finally! Before any change to our business development strategy or structure can even begin, we must take some time to really "drill down" into our existing overall company offerings and culture and honestly consider the answers to some really hard questions. The best way to do that is to ask the people that really know the answers: clients and employees.

What Do Your Clients Say?

Let's start with clients. As part of our mission to advocate for the customer, we must listen to their needs and suggestions. Give them a voice. Why? Because a great customer experience is the greatest differentiator known to man. How do we get there?

One way to accomplish this is by looking at your company, brand, products, and service offerings through what is known as the "customer lens." When the client looks at your website or brochure, calls to get assistance or a question answered, or even drives by and looks at your building, what do they see? What do they think? What do they tell others?

 The strongest factor in how a client views your company is *emotion*. How they feel when they interact with your company is the key element to client loyalty.

Ask employees to consider these two simple thoughts whenever they interact with a customer: (1) What are their emotions? Are they angry with the company? Happy? Excited? (2) What are their needs? Technical? Informational? By understanding the customer's emotions and needs, an employee will be in a better position to build an emotional attachment. Give employees a way or a place to log those thoughts—on your intranet or CRM (customer relationship management) or even a Dropbox™. Assign someone to manage that data and share it with the BD team.

Another way to collect this information from the client is through surveys. Surveys are simple and easy, but they are also inappropriate sometimes. It greatly depends on the situation. With products and general services, it works quite well. But with professional services like legal or engineering, the relationship the team member has with the client can be much more personal. The client getting a survey from corporate can feel strange or even backfire. Use good judgment based on your unique situation.

If you do choose to use the survey method, a successful gauge of client satisfaction is an industry standard metric called Net Promoter Score (NPS). Net Promoter Score is a single question survey that is sent to customers to obtain a barometer of their satisfaction level with your company. The

149

survey asks clients one simple question: "Rank how likely you would be to recommend the company to a colleague or a friend on a scale of 0–10." Their responses are divided into three categories:

1. *Promoters (9–10)*: They like your company quite a lot and would highly recommend you to others. (This is the desired response, of course!)

2. *Passives (7–8)*: They're satisfied but neutral about your company.

3. *Detractors (0–6)*: They don't like you; they really don't like you.

Send your NPS survey out on a regular basis for consistency, typically every three to six months. There are a variety of ways to send this out using tools like SurveyMonkey® or Constant Contact®, or you can simply have marketing create something customized and send it out via any social media outlet. Don't overcomplicate it or make it difficult for the client to respond. Once you have their responses, you can calculate your score by subtracting the percentage of detractors from the percentage of promoters.

Industry data and statistics are great, and someone on the BD team should always stay abreast of key performance industry indicators, but asking opinions and listening to your clients is much more important and productive. It's about real feedback.

A good friend of mine works for a medium-sized technology services firm that provides telephone, internet, and even mobile services to businesses. In the early 2000s he initiated a program to invite his company's top ten clients to lunch. Once a month he would invite one client to bring their entire local team to a popular restaurant as an appreciation luncheon. He invited *not his sales folks* but the customer service team that supported the client's employees every day. During the lunch, both teams would openly share the things that worked well and the things that really bugged them. Then, as a debrief, his staff would compare notes, and improvements would be made that better served that client. The result was solid growth and sustained client loyalty.

My friend's company was small and local, which allowed for such a personal touch. Obviously if you are a national Fortune 100, the challenge is much more complex. But the concept is exactly the same. Figure out a way to get feedback from the users of your product or service. Ask them and be willing to listen. Blogs, surveys, contests, and appreciation events are just a few of the ways this can be accomplished—but be creative. Be proactive, not reactive. Ask your customer what they think before they vote with their feet. How are we doing, and what can we do better? How was your experience?

The absolute best source for research and development of future products and services comes from this feedback. Listening to and evaluating what customers say they need and want will do a couple of things. First, it will allow you to modify the existing company offerings immediately. What do we offer that nobody wants or cares about? Second, it provides insight into new offerings that maybe you haven't thought of yet that could be invented, patented, and sold to future clients. Listen to your customers' wisdom, even if you don't want to.

Companies like FedEx and Amazon spend millions trying to capture this information for a reason. Knowing what customers really want from you and what is working and what is not, then adjusting your business development strategy is the key to client loyalty and long-term success.

What Do Your Employees Say?

Next is feedback from your employees. How do they feel about the company and what you sell? Have you even asked them? Do the same thing you do for your clients with your employees. Look at your company and all its splendor through the "employee lens."

So many companies, especially in the United States, fail to tap the largest and most accurate resource of client information at their disposal: their employees. People want to feel that they contribute. No one knows the true perception of customers better than the employees that work with them every day. Give employees a method to share their ideas. Provide them a vehicle to escalate client complaints and suggestions. Use surveys or create a page on the company intranet and then assign someone to "own" it and ensure that issues get addressed. Ask employees what they think you do well. What do you need to improve upon? As you perform the due diligence needed to evaluate your business development strategy, input and feedback from your most valuable resource is paramount.

EVER FIRED A CLIENT?

We said in *Figure 1: The Four Truths of Business Development* that business development is an endeavor that *must* be mutually beneficial to both you and your client. Too many times we are focused on "the client is always right," or we are so full of fear that if we lose a client, we will never replace them, or others will leave too. These things are simply not true. What you do or provide has value, or you would not be in business. And if you are sincerely trying to provide quality to your clients, 99 percent of them will appreciate that and be loyal and respectful.

However, there will always be that 1 percent that does not. They abuse or berate your staff regularly. They refuse to pay on time or always find some reason to reject an invoice. They abuse your warranty policies. They insist on terms and conditions that are so one-sided you are exposed to more risk than is reasonable. For whatever reason, that client has become a liability. One of my favorite sayings is, "You are either part of the solution or part of the problem." If you deem a client to be such a liability, then let them go—with respect, grace, and professionalism, of course. You can let them know that your culture and theirs simply do not mesh.

This may seem counterintuitive to all we have said about the customer experience so far, but it's not. The wrong types of customers can consume resources, destroy morale, and dilute the potential to help other clients, reducing the positive experience for the other 99 percent long term.

CREATE A BUSINESS DEVELOPMENT STRATEGY

Tactics without strategy is the noise before defeat. (Sun Tzu)[47]

P reparation is the key. A good strategy is, in my mind, preparing to win. Whenever my wife and I get ready to paint a room, she wants to just get out the paint and brush and go at it. I insist that we tape off the areas in the room we don't want painted, put down drop cloths, and lightly sand where needed. The result is always better. However, it usually takes about as long to prep as it does to paint. But a job done right is all about the preparation.

In 1985 I became a member of the Professional Association of Diving Instructors (P.A.D.I.) and eventually worked up to assistant instructor. One of the other instructors I worked with had a T-shirt he used to wear that said, "Plan the Dive, Dive the Plan." Words we all lived by every time we got in the water, literally.

---

47. Sun Tzu, *The Art of War*, written around 700 B.C. https://www.goodreads.com/book/show/10534.The_Art_of_War. Public domain.

The movie *The Hunt for Red October* was a 1990 megahit film about the USSR's best submarine captain in their newest sub who violated orders and headed for the USA. Not sure of the exact verbiage, but one of my favorite lines from the movie goes something like this: "What's his plan, son? Russians don't take a dump without a plan." I cannot count the number of times this phrase has been said during strategy and planning sessions over the years, and it always brings laughter. But the truth is there is great wisdom in these examples.

 A goal without a plan is just a wish. For us to have the optimum business development engine, first we must develop the strategy to employ for success and then develop a tactical plan to help achieve that success.

For any business to succeed, savvy business leaders typically create an overall business plan that maps out the initiatives, challenges, and markets, and how they intend to operate before just charging off blindly "into the wind," hoping for the best.

Of the many business plans and companies that I have looked at over the years, the ones that turned out to be the most successful are the ones that are focused on why they are in business and what they do best. As I pointed out earlier, in the research that he did for his book, *Good to Great*, Jim Collins found that the main reason certain companies become great is they narrowed down the focus of the company to their specific field of core competence. Again, trying to be too many things to any and all potential clients tends to dilute resources and create chaos. Be strategically focused.

According to a 2015 study performed by a renowned consulting firm, of over four thousand senior business executives surveyed, more than 50 percent said they felt their company did not have a winning business development strategy.[48] Furthermore, the survey also claimed that of the executives surveyed, nine out of ten confessed they were missing major opportunities in their markets because of that lack of strategy for winning clients. Developing goals, strategies, and tactics demands leaders think strategically but have the ability to think tactically as well. The 2015 survey also shared that of the business executives surveyed, only 8 percent excelled at both strategy *and* tactics (execution).

The line between strategy and tactics is not always so clear. In the BD strategic planning process, there are three basic questions to help us clarify:

1. What are we going to do?

2. Why are we doing it?

3. How are we going to accomplish it?

The first two questions—what and why—are the basis for setting goals and strategic planning. Once we know these answers, then and only then can we answer the last question, how. *How* makes up our tactical plan. Something like this:

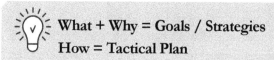

What + Why = Goals / Strategies
How = Tactical Plan

STRATEGIC PLANNING

In the same general vein as the overall company business plan, there needs to be a strategy of business development: a strategic business development plan. This plan should be focused, defined, and clearly communicated to the business

48. Paul Leinwand, Cesare Mainardi & Art Kleiner, "Only 8% of Leaders Are Good at Both Strategy and Execution," *HarvardBusinessReview.com*, 2015. Retrieved from https://hbr.org/2015/12/only-8-of-leaders-are-good-at-both-strategy-and-execution.

development team and everyone involved. This document does not need to be a thousand pages with cost projections, EBITDA, and tons of details and fine print, but a simple "road map" of what you intend to sell or not sell and to whom, what you intend to accomplish and achieve, and why these targets make sense. There should also be metrics and key performance indicators (KPIs) that are simple and concise.

One of the biggest mistakes BD leaders make when doing this is that they get too bogged down in "the weeds." Strategy is not operational planning. Again, strategy is what and why, and tactical is about how.

The plan should consist of three levels:

A. Goal

1. Strategies (for that goal)

i. Tactics (to accomplish each strategy)

You may have as many goals as you like, but the best plans try and limit them to between three and five. Too many goals in a five-year strategic plan can confuse, consume, and dilute resources. Goals should be "30,000-feet"—or overall big picture view—objectives that the thought leaders of the company agree on. Here are some general examples for goals to set:

- Increase sales by 30 percent.
- Provide the best possible work culture and professional development atmosphere for employees.
- Open in a new region or country.
- Expand existing customer base into a new product.
- Introduce a new product or service.

- Increase market share by 25 percent.

- Establish your brand in another market.

- Improve customer loyalty by 50 percent.

A great goal might be to improve customer satisfaction by 30 percent. But if that goal is improving customer satisfaction by using Bluetooth headsets in lieu of wired ones, then you have missed the point. That would be a *tactic*. Operational planning and the associated tactics are required exercises in any sound business plan for certain, but defining the goals, strategies, and tactics with a timeline and measurable key performance indicators (KPIs) is the key to creating a winning business development strategy. This strategy should be about vision. Here is an example of a sales-oriented goal:

Goal #1

Achieve $100MM in gross sales by FY 2030 through profitable growth and strategic initiatives.

Strategy #1

Expand market share in the eastern region by 25 percent.

Tactic #1

Host five lunch and learn sessions with existing clients in that region annually.

Tactic #2

Adopt one new client innovation from client feedback and ideas.

Tactic #3

Reach out to ten new clients per week in the eastern region.

Multiple strategies and multiple tactics per goal is great. Just remember there is no need to make it complex. Successful strategic planning converts complex into simple.

It is also very important to be flexible. Strategy is a wonderful thing, but circumstances, markets, and the needs of clients and employees change. Being rigid and sticking to a strategy as the competitive marketplace changes can be disastrous. A good business development strategy is dynamic and humble. What was a good idea five years ago may not be the best idea today or for the future. Develop a strategic BD plan, then revisit that plan every year and evaluate the metrics established. Adjust course as needed.

In the 1990s, International Paper Company's (IP) leadership decided to make a bold, strategic course correction. IP had been a leader in the manufacturing of white bond paper (writing and printing) and newsprint material for the prolific periodical industry for many years. People used a lot of these two products, and it was apparently quite lucrative for IP. But the world was changing. These visionary strategists observed that the consumer marketplace was moving away from so much print and into the digital space. In addition, more and more people were shopping online, ordering a wide variety of goods from places like Amazon and eBay, and every single item needed a box. So, what did they do? International Paper began to slowly sell, shut down, and repurpose its facilities in an effort to move away from bond paper and newsprint. Instead, their new strategic direction for the future would be to focus on high growth fluff pulp, container board, and corrugated "cardboard" products.[49] *Hmm. I wonder if that was a good idea?*

The point is to decide on a strategy for the future and write it down. Consider things like,

---

49. This example from IP is my own recollection of IP history.

- What does my target client look like?

- Where do I see my company in one year, five years, or ten years?

- What will success look like?

- Why are these good targets?

- What is my approach for developing new opportunities?

- Will it be mostly through expanding existing clients or new ones?

- What about new markets? New services?

- What am I willing to spend? (Develop a strategic budget.)

- Where is my core business going to come from in the future?

- What do I need to stop doing?

- What process or cultural improvements do I need to make?

. . . or any other relevant and thought-provoking questions. How far into the future should you consider strategically? That's always relative to the type of business you are in, but typically most businesses do three-, five-, or ten-year strategic documents and revisit every year. My preference is the five-year plan. Create a document that outlines the business development strategy, and create some measurable goals. There are a multitude of templates available online and a host of examples to follow. No need to overcomplicate the process. The key power points here are as follows:

1. Create a business development strategy and associated plan.

2. Share it with all your stakeholders.

3. Develop a strategic budget.

4. Revisit and refresh the document periodically.

If this task seems a little daunting, don't feel alone. The vast majority of mid-market B2B companies have no defined business development strategy at all. Either they don't see the value or it is simply something they don't know how to do, so they ignore it. Regardless of your reason, get moving on a plan.

One of the best and simplest strategic planning sessions I have ever had the good fortune to be involved with yielded three fundamental strategic goals (there is that power of three again) that clearly defined the culture, vision, and values of that company. The three simple goals we all agreed upon (using the company's vision and mission statement as a guide) were as follows:

1. TO CARE—for our employees' personal and professional growth, providing the nurturing, training, tools, and mentoring required to be of optimum value to our clients.

2. TO SERVE—our clients, existing and new, with the best people, solutions, products, and services our company can offer.

3. TO STEWARD—the income, profit, and resources, both professional and financial, afforded to us to maintain the integrity and long-term security of our company.

For each goal, a list of strategies and specific tactics were developed to achieve these goals. If you are not sure where to begin, these three basic but all-encompassing goals are a great starting point.

STRATEGIC BUDGETING

Another critical element as a part of the process of strategic business development planning is to create a strategic budget. You would be surprised at how many companies get all fired up to make change and develop a plan to pursue more business but never consider that this effort costs money.

 Creating a plan without any funding is a serious waste of time and energy.

This strategic budget and the allocated resources to execute the business development plan puts the company in a position to achieve goals and targets.

Once you have determined what you intend to focus on in your strategic business development plan, put budget numbers to each tactic, and determine what it will take to accomplish these tasks. Assign an importance level to each, and then determine from where and when the money will be available. If the cost is significant, especially in a small business, prioritize each item, then create a "rollout" plan and a timeline. Bear in mind that there will be some elements and items on the plan that can be carried out without any apparent costs or significant budget expenditure required. Items like a monthly employee meeting to share company sales progress or creating a new blog on the company website—these may have an effective zero budget number, but regardless, each should be included within the budget for tracking. Remember, these items can still have an internal cost even if it is in lost billing time for employees at the meeting or the time your marketing team spent internally updating the website for the blog.

Change is critical, but not at the cost of putting the financial health of the company at risk. It is perfectly acceptable to implement these changes in waves or milestones over a period of time.

STEP 4:

DEVELOP A TACTICAL PLAN

If I had 5 minutes to chop down a tree, I would spend the first 3 minutes sharpening my axe. (Abraham Lincoln)[50]

O nce the self-analysis is completed, clients' and employees' opinions have been engaged, and a strategic business development plan is created, it is time to consider "how" to tactically execute these goals. What people, technology, and resources will be required? What needs to be considered? What is most important? What will yield the best results?

The following items are a macro-level overview of things to consider when developing a tactical plan. Needs will differ. There is no "one size fits all" here either. Some organizations like online product companies will be much more focused on digital presence and internet marketing, where professional services companies will be more centered around physical sales presence.

---

50. https://quoteinvestigator.com/2014/03/29/sharp-axe/#more-8542.

> ☀ **Customize the plan around the market you serve.**

Although marketing, sales, and customer service are all interdependent upon the others for success, the tactical tools and resources for each will be quite different. Let's address these one at a time.

MARKETING

Create a Marketing Plan: The PIE

We already know that marketing is a very complex endeavor, and we have already outlined the importance of developing a strategic budget. Companies spend billions on marketing; some spend very little on marketing. Some don't really understand marketing at all. Some companies have no idea what is spent or if it even helps.

Regardless, the hardest piece of the Tactical Marketing Plan is the budget. What is spent, how it is spent, and what is working best will determine success or failure of the initiatives. Simplify the complex. Think of the marketing budget as a pie. As shown in the hypothetical example in *Figure 5*, the marketing program budget has many slices. Remember the strategic plan defined what our target client looks like. The size of the slices will depend on the best way to get the message of value to the targeted client. Simple. How much to dedicate to each slice will be a function of the market you are in and a leadership decision.

Sample BD Marketing Budget

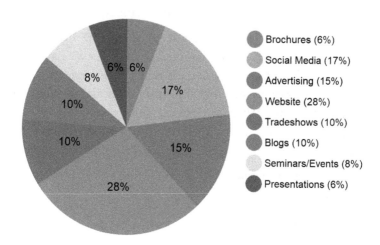

Figure 5: Sample Marketing Budget

To help, here are some general statistics from a 2018 CMO published survey:

- B2B product companies spend about 6.4 percent of *total revenue* on marketing.
- B2B service firms spend about 6.8 percent.
- Manufacturing companies devote only 2.7 percent.
- Technology/Software companies devote nearly 10 percent.
- On average, 41 percent of total marketing budget is allocated to online/digital efforts.[51]

Remember, this "pie" is a living and dynamic thing. As you move forward, tracking data and information regarding

---

51. Paraphrased from this report: "Highlights and Insights Report," *The CMO Survey*, 2018. Retrieved from https://cmosurvey.org/wp-content/uploads/sites/15/2018/02/The_CMO_Survey-Highlights_and_Insights_Report-Feb-2018.pdf.

which slices have the best and worst results will allow you to adjust budgeting course along the way.

Spend the Budget: Deliver the Message

Next, what is the best way to spend the budget and deliver the message to the targeted clients? As we have said, make an effort to prioritize each item. There are a host of effective tactics to get the attention of both existing and potential clients. What is best for any given company will again be specific to the industry and product/service you deliver. Here are just a few of the most popular venues:

- Social media
- Webinars
- Telephone campaigns
- Email campaigns
- Direct "snail mail" campaigns (somewhat outdated)
- Expert speaker/deliver a white paper at events
- Subject matter content on blog sites
- Brochures and material content downloadable from website
- Print and digital advertising
- Conferences, trade shows, and events
- Free consultation or evaluation offers

Allow me to reiterate a point from Part 1 that is vastly overlooked by most B2B companies that are spending their marketing dollars in the wrong way. If 80 percent of company revenue comes from existing clients, then why spend less than 20 percent of your marketing budget on the 80 percent revenue contributors? The constant obsession with new client acquisition is healthy and great and how companies grow, I agree. But it is amazing how blind marketing teams are to the need for maintaining, nurturing, and growing the current client base. If this is a new concept and you are not sure how the split should look, start out by using a 50/50 rule. Focus 50 percent of the marketing budget on the existing clients and adjust from there.

Develop the Marketing Team

Most marketing teams will vary greatly in size, depending on the budget, industry, and effort required. Develop a winning team structure that fits the company. Some typical role descriptions could be as follows:

- *VP/Director/Marketing Manager:* Accountable for the leadership and development of people, marketing collateral, proposals, social media, CRM, advertising, PR, client campaigns, client events, and any/all aspects of brand management. Responsible for the empowerment, mentoring, and direct supervision of all marketing staff.

- *Proposal and Media Coordinator:* Responsible for the development and/or oversight of *all* corporate proposals, RFQs, and RFPs. Will have ownership of the library that will include resumes, project sheets, descriptive paragraphs, and information required to assemble all proposals.

- *Graphic Designer:* Accountable for the development of designs and content for public relations, advertising, website content, brochure and collateral development, and all marketing programs as defined by management.

- *CRM/Social Media Administrator:* Own and be responsible for the corporate CRM. This will include serving as system administrator, user trainer, and report manager.

- *Marketing Assistants:* Report to the marketing manager and support the team in a variety of ways.
- *Website Designers:* Own the website and all web presence. Responsible for layout, SEO (search engine optimization), content insertion and blog management, metrics, and continuous refresh of the site.

This is a great place to remind ourselves that each person on the marketing team is part of the business development chain. Any chain is only as strong as its weakest link. Putting someone in a position because they do not fit anywhere else in the company or because they are a friend of the family—without the right skills—is an injustice to the rest of the team, the company, and the client. Many smaller companies fail to understand the value this team provides. Don't make that mistake.

Telesales/Telemarketing

Telesales and telemarketing are very similar and are techniques that play a part in any tactical approach to delivering the message. Like most consumers, I am disgusted by telemarketers calling me and trying to sell me insurance or timeshares while I am trying to eat dinner. The truth is that if this technique did not work well, companies would not dedicate so much energy to it and spend millions of dollars on telemarketing and telesales.

This technique is about volume and numbers. In Part 1 we discussed Rule 122. A good telesales representative will make one hundred calls to get twenty people of interest to close two deals. As previously discussed, this Rule 122 or 100/20/2 strategy has been employed for decades and is really quite effective in the consumer arena and many B2B applications. Some companies use "inside sales" staff to reach out to existing customers to share new programs, better services, or even a new product. Others use this technique to "cold call" potential clients to try and qualify them as leads to be followed up by sales staff. Should this function be a part of customer service? Marketing? Sales? That depends on what the outcome is for the initiative. In most cases, this is a marketing function. Remember the definition of marketing: delivering the message to qualified masses.

Unlike consumer selling, however, in the B2B world, this telesales concept is somewhat limited. Qualifying people on the phone in an attempt to set a meeting or to gain an appointment is a staple of any good salesperson. As a BDM (business development manager) I have used telephone cold calling many times with great results. But allow me to confess that it is absolutely brutal and grueling to make one hundred cold calls in a day, attempting to,

- deliver the ninety second elevator speech,

- determine if someone has interest,

- identify potential pain points, and

- try to set an appointment.

But it does work. "Warm calls" and referrals are much more effective and easier, but in some cases, you simply have to pick up the phone and start dialing.

Engaging a Public Relations Firm

Several times we have mentioned the value of public relations. Many B2B companies that do not have dedicated public relations staff engage a public relations agency when they want to protect, enhance, or build their reputations through the media.

 A good agency partner can help analyze the company, find the positive messages, and translate those messages into positive media content.

CRACKING THE BUSINESS DEVELOPMENT CODE

This message of value that is transmitted to new and existing clients must be concise, tailored, and effective. Using a professional to help craft those messages is always a great approach.

However, these consulting services are not cheap and demand precious resources from the marketing budget. Highly competitive industries use public relations experts to create a competitive advantage or differentiating factors to set them apart. The value that such an effort would bring to your company is very subjective and depends greatly on the industry, service, or product your company provides. Be wise and prudent with the use of such services and how it may fit into your marketing strategy and budget.

Hiring the right team members for the right jobs on the marketing team is the first step in a strong marketing initiative. Giving them a budget and allowing them to develop a sound "go to market" plan is the second. Whenever I have created teams in the past, I have always tried to surround myself with people who are experts in their field and a lot smarter than me, then I give them what they need so *we all* can succeed.

 Regardless of what industry your company is in, marketing plays a vital role in successful growth.

Many companies, when sales begin to slow down, look to sales and marketing as the first place to reduce staff. This is a short-term solution to cash flow but most certainly a longer-term tactical mistake. Remember that in Henry Ford's day, they referred to all things involving marketing as *advertising*. But his message is still spot on.

172

Stopping advertising to save money is like stopping your watch to save time. (Henry Ford)

SALES

Simplify: Make It Easy

Next up is the sales portion of the tactical plan. Typically, technical competence and the best products are considered to be the greatest advantage in sales.

 But the truth is that unless you offer something that customers cannot buy anywhere else, simplicity and reduced complexity are the real advantage in today's sales market. Make it easy to buy from your company.

Amazon makes it easy to search, click, and buy. If you have an issue, then send it back, and they will pay for the shipping. Wayfair took that a step further and provides free shipping for delivery and returns.

The takeaway is, don't make it difficult to do business with your firm. What creative way can your company make doing business with you fun, easy, painless, and fruitful?

Create a Sales Funnel

For what seems like eternity, every salesperson or sales manager has talked about the "sales funnel" (see *Figure 6*). There are thousands of variations on this theme. Tons of books, papers, and seminars have spun this time-tested method of monitoring the sales process in every conceivable way, so there is no need to explain or drill down in detail. It is really quite simple.

Figure 6: Sales Funnel

Salespeople take leads and convert them into *maybes*. Leads can come from marketing calls, website blogs, referrals from clients, and a host of various places. Some are a good fit; some are not. Some will want what the company can offer; some will not. The ones that fit become *prospects*. These are the cream, the gold, the potential clients that get the most attention from the sales staff, because this is the group most likely to need the solutions the company can offer. What are their problems? How can we help? All the "pain point" stuff that is part of a great sales relationship.

The mission is to turn as many prospects into loyal clients as possible. No magic or secret sauce. Monitoring, tracking, and keeping up with all this activity is the responsibility of the CRM. The only secret is to ensure the information on a potential client's journey is captured in the CRM in a way that is easy to use and to share this data among the marketing, sales, and customer service staff. If it is not easy to input, retrieve, and report on, then it becomes worthless as a tool. *Make it easy!*

Make the complicated simple. If you must have a PhD in computer science to perform any of these CRM tasks, then the energy and the investment are wasted.

Define Channels

The next step is to define the ways in which to generate sales leads for the funnel. This should always be a combination of marketing, sales, and sales support efforts. Here are some typical sales avenues, but by no means is this an exhaustive list:

- *Customer Service:* Leads for new services, new products, or upgrades from the existing client base is by far the best channel. Direct and frequent internal interaction between the trilogy players is critical but is also the most often overlooked resource. Referrals to other companies from existing clients is the number one referral source for new clients as well.

- *Inbound Leads:* Leads generated from a website, banners, or other such mass media offers.

- *Advertising:* Leads generated by billboards, print ads, digital and search engine advertising.

- *Social Media Advertising:* Leads generated by social media advertising like Facebook or LinkedIn.

- *Outbound Leads:* Leads generated by initiatives like targeted email prospecting, cold calls, and direct campaigns.

- *Referrals:* Leads that are referred by satisfied customers.

- *Networking:* Leads resulting from trade shows, events, delivering subject matter presentations, and sponsorships.

- *Cross-Sells:* Leads from existing clients. This is the most commonly overlooked avenue of leads. If the company offers a variety of products or services, these are opportunities to cross-sell new products/ services to existing clients. Cross-selling of services and products to existing clients is the quickest and possibly the strongest revenue source of all.

Engage Employees as Sales

Leads also come from employees, if we are willing to listen and act. Remember that everyone in the company is a salesperson.

In the mid-2000s, I was leading the business development effort for an industrial services group. One day the corporate operations safety manager had been reading his daily industry information stream online (every job function has periodicals, blogs, and web-based sites they watch) and noticed an industrial company that was not a client yet had recently been tagged with a host of safety violations. The violations cost the company severely. Our team did some research and found the environmental health and safety (EHS) manager for the facility and reached out. We met and were able to secure a contract to assist with the compliance issue within the facility. Never underestimate the worth of empowered employees.

Identify Sales Support/Enablement

Sales support is a term that has been around for a very long time and one we have discussed in detail already. It is not a new function in any way. It refers to a variety of tasks that help sales be more successful. Today there are a host of catchy names for this function, as we discussed in Part 1: sales enablement, customer advocacy, and so on. The name is unimportant, but the role has always been critical.

These functions differ per company, industry, and team, but dedicate the right employees to provide support to the sales team. Having skilled support staff is paramount to the overall success of the sales operation.

Focus

Developing clearly defined target markets is essential for any business development tactical plan. Focus is the key to success. Time is money. Without a definitive target market or demographic in mind, companies can wander around, aimlessly prospecting.

What does focus do for the tactical sales team?

- The focused tactical sales approach allows you to qualify and prioritize, making the best use of limited sales and marketing resources.

- Focused target markets and potential client definitions allow for the creation of specific content and clearer knowledge of potential client needs.

- The focused tactical approach also better defines what products and services best suit the chosen target clients.

 Take time to define and refine the list of companies, industries, and markets by name that you intend to target. Write them down.

Initiate a Go/No-Go Process

This is something many companies fail to do properly if they even give it a second thought at all. Not all decisions will require a structured process, but by having a process, leadership sends a clear signal that can help the decision-making team say "no" when "no" is the correct answer, and can help to ensure that no opportunity that might be right for the company is missed.

As part of the process, each significant sales proposal, RFQ/RFP opportunity and project pursuit should be subject to a structured *go/no-go* outline prior to pursuit. Criteria for acceptance should be developed. There are a variety of structured processes to use that can be found online. One common, time-tested favorite is TAS (Target Account Selling). TAS asks questions like,

- Is there a real opportunity?
- Can we compete?
- Can we win?
- Do we have the right resources right now?
- Is it worth winning?

It is also perfectly acceptable to create a customized, unique decision matrix, depending upon the industry with which the company is associated. Regardless, this should be a "pass" or "fail" process, incorporating a committee of relevant stakeholders consisting of marketing, sales, customer service, and operations. Investing time into pursuits costs real money. Not all pursuits make sense. The important thing is if the criteria is not met and a "fail" or *no-go* decision is reached, the decisions must be documented and communicated to all stakeholders, including the potential client.

CUSTOMER SERVICE

With 80 percent of the company's annual revenue coming from the existing, loyal client base, the third and potentially the most important part of the tactical business development plan—customer service—is really about two things: customer retention and expanding relationships.

Ensure Customer Retention

Very few companies focus on or even track customer retention as a part of their business development plan. How many customers did your company lose last year? To whom? Why? Statistics vary from industry to industry, but,

 On average, it costs about six times more to acquire a new customer than it does to keep existing ones.

So if a company generates $20 million a year in new relationships and subsequent sales but loses $5 million in existing revenue from lost clients, that company is actually losing revenue and going backwards.

The metric for client retention is client retention rate. Customer or client retention rate (CRR) is a measure of how well any given company or division is performing toward true long-term client success. How is CRR calculated? There are many ways to calculate CRR, but here is the most popular. Say XYZ company has 5,000 existing clients on January 1st, and on January 31st the total is down to 4,800. But XYZ also adds 200 new clients during that same month. Here is the calculation:

 Client Retention Rate = (C – N) / E

C = Number of total clients at the end of January
N = Number of new clients during January
E = Number of clients January 1st

This calculation incorporates the number of clients remaining at the end of January without counting the number of new customers acquired.

$$(4{,}800 - 200) / 5{,}000 = .92$$

or

$$.92 \times 100 = 92\% \text{ Client Retention Rate}$$

In a perfect world, companies would like the CRR to reach 100 percent, which means that they never lose a single customer. That's not reality. Your number is pursuant to your company, but aiming for 90 percent or at the very least 85 percent CRR is reasonable. Again, this will vary from industry to industry. Great companies track this rate and try and improve upon it every month.

Encourage Customer Relationship Expansion

In recent years, in an effort to both combat the loss of existing clients and focus on expanding relationships, many companies have created the positions discussed in Part 1 of the trilogy. These positions we mentioned, such as customer success agent, sales enablement manager, client engagement manager, customer experience manager, etcetera, are great signs of the customer relationship revolution. Each of these roles has the primary purpose of improving the experience of both existing and newly acquired customers.

Client loyalty means a couple of things. First and most obvious, it ensures that the current revenue stream should be steady and reliable. Great news! But second and equally as important is it affords companies with truly loyal clients to both expand the number of products or services existing clients buy, while at the same time being provided referrals for new business from the friends of these loyal clients. This is the least expensive, fastest, and most effective way to grow your business.

These tactics and positions just mentioned should reside in the customer service segment of the organization in order to be most effective. But,

 Ensuring that fluid and frequent communication fostering true collaboration with the associated salesperson is paramount.

This is how the client will see a unified company when they view through that "client lens" described in Step 2.

CONCLUSION

The purpose of this segment is not for it to be a detailed, step-by-step guide to follow in order to reinvent or create the optimum recipe, or a "how to" book for business development tactical organizational structure. There are many outstanding authors who have created mountains of wonderful "how to" advice on these tactics. The main purpose herein is to share experience and observations regarding how marketing, sales, and customer service have become too separated and actually compete within companies and how to get back on track.

If the skill set to create your own tactical plan does not reside inhouse, there are many very credible consulting firms that can assist with the development and execution monitoring of a comprehensive tactical plan. Do not hesitate to ask for help. If it is financially feasible, using a third-party professional facilitator during the process of developing the strategic business development plan and associated tactics will yield better results than trying to do this on your own.

181

STEP 5:

EXAMINE THE ORGANIZATIONAL STRUCTURE

Organizational health is the single greatest competitive advantage in any business. (Patrick Lencioni)[52]

At one point or another we have all heard the phrase, "You can't get there from here." As we pointed out earlier, most companies find their organizational structure is a significant barrier to getting to their revenue or corporate growth goal because of an ineffective business development engine.

Growth stimulates complexity. The introduction of technology and global enterprise has been a real game changer in the past few decades. Adding organizational structure and new departments to keep pace with global growth is perfectly normal in business, but ensuring the business development engine is aligned for the best possible client outcome is a real challenge.

---

52. Patrick Lencioni, *The Advantage: Why Organizational Health Trumps Everything Else in Business* (San Francisco, CA: Jossey-Bass, 2012).

We are all subject to the thoughts Charles E. Hummel outlined in his book *Tyranny of the Urgent*. In his text, he suggests that really important things can get crowed out by what we think is urgent. *Urgent* and *busy* do not mean "efficient" and "focused."[53]

 Strive to convert complex and complicated into simple.

The next step is about looking at your current company and management structure and evaluating how well suited you are to the trilogy concepts. The idea is not to spend countless hours drilling down into each group and sub-group but to simply assess if there may be some internal barriers present. So let's cruise up to thirty thousand feet and look down upon your organization.

Organizational Chart
(Typical Structure)

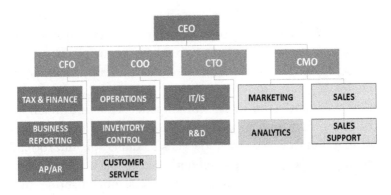

Figure 7: Organizational Chart—Typical Structure

53. Charles E. Hummel, *Tyranny of the Urgent* (Madison, WI: InterVarsity Christian Fellowship, 1967).

Here is an example of a typical corporate structure. In *Figure 7* we can clearly see that customer service is a function of operations and is distinctly and operationally separated from sales or marketing. Different divisions, different groups, and different management mentalities. I am by no means implying that the treatment of clients by operations staff would be wrong or less than acceptable. However, with this organizational divide, the chance that future and new selling opportunities never get shared with sales is very high. Many times I have heard salespeople say that once a client is landed and the initial order is taken, then it is the responsibility of customer service to take care of their needs. That sales' job is to go out and find more clients.

This is a "silo" mentality that breeds separation. This mindset is fatal to long-term client success.

Organizational Chart
(Recommended)

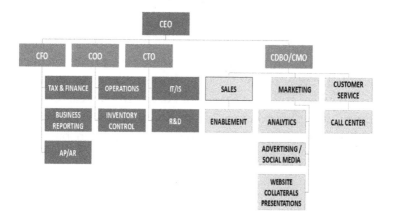

Figure 8: Organizational Chart—Recommended

In *Figure 8* we see a different organization. Customer service is now under the umbrella of the chief revenue or chief business development officer. This allows for continuity of information exchange and keeps the ownership of customer happiness or success in the same downline.

Obviously these figures do not cover all companies and the unique structural needs that will apply. What works for an engineering consulting firm would not work for an electronics component manufacturer. However, the general takeaway should be the same, regardless of how complex or straightforward your company may be. There is no magic structure that is the "end all." The titles that show up in the boxes are really unimportant. The point is that if we view our organization through that "client lens" we discussed in Step 2, we might see a company that has the potential to be dysfunctional.

Again, strive to convert complex and complicated into simple. Why?

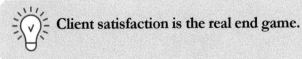 **Client satisfaction is the real end game.**

So step back, sketch a picture of your structure, and be open minded in your review. Can your business development team get to where you want to go from here? In our zeal to create the optimum accounting and operationally efficient machine, did we forget about the reason we are really in business? Helping our clients succeed.

STEP 6:

EVALUATE THE BUSINESS DEVELOPMENT TEAM

Get the right people on the bus, the wrong people off the bus, and the right people in the right seats. (Jim Collins)[54]

We know that evaluating the company structure is key to success. Equally important is the evaluation of the people within that structure and how each person fits into the puzzle. As we have said over and over, people are our greatest asset. People make any business. Therefore having the right people in the right roles is essential.

In business today we would be hard pressed to find anyone that has not heard the saying, "Get the right seat on the bus." But what exactly does that mean, and how does it apply to my business development team?

I am a fan of Jim Collins. Mostly I am a fan of the years of detailed and painstaking research his team undertook and the conclusions they revealed in his classic 2001 book, *Good*

---

54. Collins, *Good to Great*, paraphrase.

to Great. In that text he told us that companies that make the leap to greatness are those that first get the right people on the bus and then figure out where to drive it. He also states that we must get the people into the right seat on that bus or they simply need to get off. I have always found this timeless concept to be accurate, regardless of the product or service being sold.

But how do we get them in "the right seat"? General Electric (GE) was one of the first companies to really engage this concept. Interestingly enough, in his book, Jim Collins did not mention GE to be one of the eleven great companies he discovered from his insanely intense research. And mistakenly, many people attribute the "right seat" concept to Jack Welch, former CEO of General Electric.

In his book, *Jack: Straight from the Gut,* Welch states GE tried numerous evaluation systems to implement the "right seat on the bus" idea and weed out poor performers. They eventually developed a program called the "Differentiation Vitality Curve."[55] This is also often referred to as the "20-70-10 rule." Managers at every level continually assess employees, and they determine which are in the coveted top 20 percent, the vital middle 70 percent, and the bottom 10 percent. Employees are either *A, B,* or *C* players.

A players are superstars or "hyper-performers"—the ones that make things happen; the employees that represent the cream of the workforce. These "superstars" also seem to have what Welch referred to as the "Four E's and a P of Leadership": energy, energize, edge, execute, and passion.

B players are the backbone of the success of a company, and good managers work to try and sustain them and help *B*s improve and become *A*s.

C players are average at best. Rather than get things done, they tend to suck the energy and motivation from those around them. *C*s need to be identified, weeded out, and/

---

55. Jack Welch, *Jack: Straight from the Gut* (NY: Warner Books, Inc., 2001).

or terminated. Now to many of us, that sounds incredibly harsh, and by today's standards, it most likely is quite strong. But understand that at the time, GE was bleeding money, and Welch needed a solution. Using this concept, and under Welch's leadership, the company's value rose over 4,000 percent from 1981 to 2001.

My version of this approach is a lot simpler. All employees and team members fall into one of three categories: red, yellow, and green players.

 Only hire green, strive to convert yellows to green, and weed out the red.

But the part of that story that gets forgotten is that Welch also went on to say that if someone is in the wrong seat on the bus, it is the company's obligation to help them find the right seat. How many people in your company are quality folks but are doing a job they don't really like or are not particularly good at doing? If a person loves numbers and accounting but for some reason has found their way onto a sales team, then the disservice is not only to the team but the individual. The responsibility of great leaders, and one of the things Welch was adamant about, was to see if there was an accounting seat available on the bus for that person. It is an obligation and a best practice. That way the company wins and the employee wins. That is the main takeaway here.

Remember the quote from Einstein: "Everybody is a genius at something. But if you judge a fish by its ability to climb a tree it will live its whole life believing that it is stupid." Well it applies here more than ever. If we can ensure that whether they are on the marketing team as a graphic designer or an account manager on the customer service team, each has the right qualities for the task we are asking them to perform, then the bus is going somewhere great.

189

This seems simple, but in real life it can be extraordinarily difficult to execute. How do we know what seat people should occupy? How do you tell what someone is really good at doing? There are many ways to accomplish that. Start by asking them. What are their passions and interests?

Have human resources conduct a survey of hobbies, skills, talents, and passions as an internal "fun" game for employees. Allow people to participate in a formal DISC profile as part of a personal development effort. DISC is a behavior assessment tool based on psychologist William Marston's theory that revolves around four different personality traits: dominance (D), influence (I), steadiness (S), and conscientiousness (C). Learning more about the employee's strengths and talents will be a huge move in the right direction.

What kinds of things should business development team members know? Obviously that depends on their specific role and which one of the three pillars they support. If the team member is responsible for website design, then that person should have the technical training and experience required for that specific job. The same goes for graphic designers, social media staffers, and parts counter sales staff. The product knowledge and technical ability to perform must be there.

But trilogy-oriented business development involves a wider-level thought process that encompasses all the elements: marketing, sales, and customer service. The team member must be more than just technically competent. Each must be in tune with the company's leadership strategy and typically understand the following types of things:

- The current state of the business itself.

- What is the company really good at providing?

- The current state of the industry in which they provide solutions and the potential future of the markets they serve.

190

- What types of communications methods are the most effective?

- Who are the main competitors, and what are they doing?

- What are the main sources of sales or revenue?

- What does the ideal customer profile look like?

- What are the potential and unexplored market opportunities?

- Where is the company primed for business expansion that complements the existing business?

- Price points: What are clients willing to pay for the product or service?

- What drives clients to the company and away from competitors?

Given the broad scope of business development and associated activities (marketing, sales, and customer service), there are endless possibilities.

 From exploring growth opportunities in existing markets, to coming up with a more efficient way to provide client feedback, everything matters under the business development umbrella.

The idea is to ensure that the right types of strategic and passionate thinkers are involved in the right areas.

My friend and colleague Matthew Waddell says all people are some combination of strategic and tactical thinkers. I believe that no one is ever 100 percent strategic or 100 percent tactical, but everyone falls somewhere in between on the "Business Thinker Scale." It has been my observation that most business folks normally fall into the "typical" zone on the scale, with a standard mix of both tactical and strategic thought (see *Figure 9*).

Business Thinker Scale
(Strategic vs. Tactical)

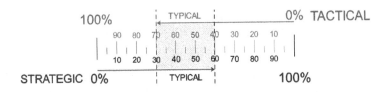

Figure 9: Business Thinker Scale

However, there are exceptions. Really talented operations people, engineers, research scientists, and project managers will be much more tactically oriented and can fall into the far right range on the scale. Conversely, people that are in the far left range are typically prone to be much more strategically minded. These are the CEOs, sales leaders, developers of new markets, long range planners, catalysts for new products, and seekers of new relationships. Neither is any better or adds more value to an organization than the other, but it is critical to recognize the different types of personalities and ensure again that they are in the right roles or "seats on the bus."

Choosing the right people to be part of the business development team from a technical skill set perspective is fairly straightforward. But picking those that have the right strategic ability and soft skills is significantly more difficult. Most soft skills (those personal attributes that enable someone to interact effectively and harmoniously with other people) can't be taught, but the ones that are most applicable to our business development team are as follows:

1. Passion and energy
2. Personal drive/self-motivated
3. Integrity and strong work ethic
4. Ability to listen and solve problems
5. Vivacity (ability to hear "no"' and bounce back)
6. Emotional and self-aware
7. Intelligent communicator
8. Positive, confident attitude
9. Team-oriented collaborator

This list was primarily targeted at sales folks, but I firmly believe it applies to anyone that is a part of the customer-facing business development engine. People that really have a vested interest in what the company does and the energy to deliver your message of value will ensure the success of the team.

Team. Team. Team. Funny how that word keeps popping up. It keeps being used over and over because business development is a team sport. In some way, everyone in the organization is a part of the business development engine.

 The primary drivers for that engine are collaboration, sharing of information, and customer-centric focus. However, reality has shown that not all employees will have the drive or zeal that is needed.

Many people simply show up and punch in. These are the folks that were previously referred to as "red" or "C" players and don't need to be on the bus. These folks can drain the life from any business development team with the four words that can stifle momentum (and should never be tolerated): "That's not my job!"

The mission is to identify those folks and help them move on to a different career.

 Everything done in business development is in some way in support of satisfying the client.

If a particular task doesn't technically fall into an employee's job description, but that person takes the responsibility to ensure that task gets done or is brought to the attention of the right person, they become part of the solution. Those are the kinds of team members we want on our bus!

One of my favorite authors, Patrick Lencioni, in his book *The Ideal Team Player*, says that the ideal person for any team should be *humble, hungry, and smart.*[56] The three essential virtues in equal measures seem to be an outstanding measuring stick when evaluating any individual player. Lencioni explains that "smart" is not referring to the individual's intellectual prowess but the person's people skills. Smart with people. Understanding how to listen to and have common sense about people. They tend to intuitively feel the dynamics in a group situation and adjust in the most effective way. It is a natural talent and one that is not easily learned. "Smart people," with this natural ability, tend to make the best business development team players.

 The right employees in the right role for the right reason are unstoppable.

---

56. Patrick Lencioni, *The Ideal Team Player* (Hoboken, NJ: Jossey-Bass, 2016).

Strive to seek out, train, support, and reward the best you can find.

 What happens if we invest in our business development team and then they leave the company? We should be much more worried about where we will be if we do not invest and they choose to stay.

STEP 7:

METRICS, TOOLS, AND SYSTEMS

If you want your business development team to succeed, give them the right tools.

I n any initiative or endeavor a company undertakes, there are always specific tools required and scorekeeping that is necessary. Good business development oversight requires these as well. The last step in this seven-step evaluation process is about the metrics, tools, and systems for a sustained and fruitful business development engine.

Throughout this text, we have repeatedly emphasized simplicity. Make the complex simple. Strive to make complicated more simplistic. Keep it simple, stupid (KISS). Step 7 should be no different.

Most CIOs[57] today would argue that the more data that can be captured the better. And to some degree that is true. Just as was outlined in the first chapter, the more that is known about clients' buying habits, signals, preferences, and desires,

---

57. CIO refers to chief information officer.

the better companies can be at predicting what they will buy next for certain. This is really applicable in the development of new products based on client need and industry feedback, as pointed out in Step 2.

 But truly successful B2B mid-market companies should not be so much about science and data manipulation as about ensuring that each team member is providing right solutions and quality products to clients.

Solving the problems that clients share.

However, in order to ensure that the business development engine is doing and performing well, a certain amount of data must be captured, utilized, and maintained. How much is enough? What is overkill? That will depend on the industry, specific market, and culture of the company.

In the age of information, collecting and maintaining too much information is what most companies do and is not necessarily a mistake. Storage and processing power are cheap; feel free to fill up as many servers as you like. The point is that regardless of how much information is or is not collected, there are some basic must-have tools and metrics for any business development engine to operate effectively and efficiently.

Although this is by no means an exhaustive list, here is a brief overview of some of the basic tools and metrics to support the trilogy pillars of business development and why they are important.

METRICS

The local sports arena in our city plays host to both professional and college basketball teams. My close friend

Gene Bailey is the statistician guy you see at the table on the sidelines and for years has diligently collected the player statistics for many a game. Like most people, I have always seen the players and team statistics just pop up on the screen and never gave much thought to how these were collected. I guess I assumed it was magic. What I learned is that a skilled "caller" like Gene calls out the activities, and a computer operator on either side of him listens to his shorthand code words, interprets them, and types them into a screen. Amazing!

Business development metrics are like keeping score. Are we winning or losing? How well are the players doing their jobs? The key element in the need for any metric should be directed at accountability. Specific and unique key performance indicators (KPIs) should be developed and maintained for each individual, department, branch, and region as it pertains to business development. Data and information captured in the business development process allows teams to manage KPI performance so surprises can be anticipated and corrected proactively. This data can also provide marketplace feedback on the effectiveness of your business development plan, allowing better focus of resources on high-performing tactics and adjustments to lesser ones that must be made.

Choose the metrics that matter to your team effort—those that contribute to generating revenue and ensuring client loyalty. What is important to one firm may not be to another. Be focused and intentional. However, allow me to insist at this point that your reports and metrics must be lean. I have seen business development teams that were unfortunately supervised by an accounting leader that had so many detailed reports and captured data elements that it was mind boggling. Most of the time I simply tossed the reports in the trash after his reporting team had spent hours upon hours assimilating the data. It was just too complex and

199

cumbersome to be helpful to a simpleton like me. Too many metrics can confuse or dilute the true reason for collecting and sharing them. Be selective with your metrics. Some will be unique to the industry or specific to your company, but there are some that are universal.

Sales and Customer Service

Strategy and tactics are essential considerations, but sustained sales growth is about managing and monitoring the numbers too. Tracking the right things and then ensuring these are communicated to the team leaders makes the task much easier.

According to a 2016 LinkedIn blog post, 74 percent of B2B companies do not track the number of monthly visits, leads, calls, or sales opportunities identified by their sales staff.[58] That is simply mind numbing and shocking to me. If it is not tracked, it cannot be measured. If it is not measured and monitored, then how will companies know if the employee is effective? When to hire more or let some go? How will leadership know if a campaign is working? If your team is one of this 74 percent, then stop whatever you are doing and immediately engage some level of metrics. Please.

Here are some examples of core metrics to use:

- New client adds/Existing clients lost
- Number of new leads/Sales calls/Visits
- Lead generation by channel
- Appointments set/Achieved
- Gross sales by $$/Gross sales by activity
- Backlog/Percent increase YOY[59]

58. Jason Miller, "50 B2B Marketing Metrics You Can Track and Improve," *LinkedIn*, 2016. Retrieved from https://business.linkedin.com/en-uk/marketing-solutions/blog/posts/B2B-Marketing/2016/50-B2B-Marketing-Metrics-You-Can-Track-and-Improve.

59. YOY refers to year-over-year.

- Sales wins by $$ and by product/Win rate
- New business vs. existing client reorder
- New hot opportunities identified
- Activities or touches by type
  » Visits
  » Emails or digital touches
  » Phone conversations
- Client retention rate
- Prospect to client conversion rate
- Actual sales as a % of net revenue
- Customer acquisition cost (CAC)
- Website hits and click throughs
- Marketing qualified leads (MQLs)
- Cost per proposal
- Actual marketing expense/Percent of net revenue
- Website content downloads
- Website forms completed
- Social media "likes" or mentions
- Net promoter score (NPS)

Just pick the ones that are important to you. Tracking both progress and failure is mandatory. However, I have also seen people that went overboard and wanted to track the number of steps salespeople took every day. Don't be ridiculous. Be sane and realistic. There are literally hundreds of valuable metrics as it may relate to marketing, sales, and customer service. Again, determine what is important to you, and be consistent in both tracking and sharing the numbers with the team. Keep it simple. Only track what is meaningful.

Share the metrics with the team. Several years ago, a technology start-up that enlisted my advice decided to create a giant thermometer graphic and place it on the wall in the breakroom. All it tracked was new client acquisition numbers. The goal at the top was five thousand new clients by year end. If the team reached that goal, then each employee got a bonus, and the company leaders had to serve banana splits to every employee. With each new client add, the "mercury" was elevated by one. Whenever any employee came into the breakroom, he or she could clearly see how the team was doing. The atmosphere at the firm was excited and stimulated because everyone knew the goal, and everyone wanted to be a cheerleader.

The point is to drive action. If metrics, good or bad, are kept on some secret report for managers' eyes only, a huge part of the point is lost.

TOOLS AND TECHNOLOGY

Determining technology needs is next in the process. In today's complex world of digital tools and global connectivity, the options and possibilities are virtually limitless. In order for any team member to be effective, the right choice and mix of digital and analog tools and/or technology is essential. Again, the best plan is to keep it simple and be smart about what is chosen.

We will go into more detail on the following pages, but here is a short list of some of the key tools that are basics for any business development engine:

- Website
- Marketing design tools
- Social media and apps
- Collaterals
- Systems and CRM software
- Devices

Website

Most companies today have a website, but there are still B2B companies that do not have a *web presence* because they think they don't sell in that space. My advice is that if you don't have a website or strong web presence, get one immediately.

 Over 75 percent of B2B buyers say digital website content significantly impacts their selection process, and 60 percent say they make an entire B2B purchase decision based on the company's website alone.

We have touched on the website in several places so far because it is really important. The company website is the flagship for marketing and typically the first contact a potential client has with any company. It is a staple. How elaborate the site is will be directly proportionate to how much money is spent and what you want it to achieve. Some companies spend a few thousand and some spend millions. There is no defined guideline for websites. Just ensure that the site is professional, easy to navigate, and clearly defines the products, services, values, and culture of the company to the client.

Having an in-house "webmaster" is the best approach because the magic and mystery that surrounds websites is exacerbated by the sheer number of experts and gurus that try and mystify those of us who don't understand. If you can't afford the luxury of a dedicated employee, then by all means find someone that you can trust. Web designers are like financial advisors; there are many that are honest and look out for the best interest of their clients, but there are an equal number that will take advantage of our lack of understanding.

The website is a cornucopia of potential priceless information and can do a multitude of functions for your business development team. The website can do things like support blogs, provide links to other items, show content that's interesting, support marketing campaigns, enhance client relationship building, foster brand awareness, and add value to virtually every element of the company's revenue generating efforts. By using search engine optimization (SEO) techniques, your website can be optimized to appear in more searches and appear more often.

I could go on for pages talking about the potential of websites, but the short version is, embrace the website and use it to your full advantage.

Marketing Design Tools

Oh, my! One thing that is certain is that in today's environment of digital design tools, software, mobile apps, wireless data, and instant communications, there are so many options for marketers, it's mesmerizing. Trying to describe them all would be fruitless for me, and you can go blind trying to learn them all. Ceros, Adobe Spark, Pixlr, Pablo, Canva, Venngage, Weld, MailChimp, Constant Contact, Piktochart, Squarespace, Infogram . . . it's endless.

But every marketing designer has a favorite. My team uses the basics: Microsoft Office Suite, Adobe Suite—InDesign and Photoshop. We also use some email campaign software and WordPress for our website. This is not an endorsement; it's just what we use.

There are better and more elaborate tools, for sure. The issue is to choose what you can afford and choose what makes the most sense for what you are trying to accomplish.

Social Media and Apps

In Part 1 we described the benefits of social media in marketing. There is no question that today and in the future social media will become the centerpiece of all marketing and possibly even become the basis for the overall business development engine for B2B companies. LinkedIn, Facebook, Twitter, Instagram, and new products yet to come can provide a ton of benefits to engage social media. For instance,

- Establishing your brand
- Increasing brand awareness
- Increasing website traffic
- Generating leads
- Promoting content
- Reputation management
- Crisis communication
- Customer and audience engagement
- Customer service and customer support
- Monitoring conversations relevant to your brand
- Learning more about your customers' needs
- Targeted advertising

Include and embrace this venue as an integral part of the marketing tools your business development team employs. If you are not engaging social media in at least a small way, do it now.

Another terrific tool in today's marketplace is the use and creation of applications for handheld devices. These "apps" cover an incredible array of possibilities—from off-the-shelf things like Google Maps to help team members with navigation, to custom-created applications to collect proprietary project data for a customer site. I am not the right guy to provide an in-depth overview of this technology, but I will say this is the future. Find someone to help you navigate this maze.

Lastly, there are texts. Texting is powerful. Texting is dangerous. I have seen more damage done to relationships with these 160 characters than any other medium, including face to face. It's emotionless conversation and can be easily misconstrued. Be careful. Look at it this way: Sending a text to someone's personal communicator in an instant manner is extremely personal. If your client relationship has reached a point where you have been trusted with the number, treat it with the utmost respect. Think before you text. You can't take it back.

On the other hand, instant messaging can be enormously effective. Last year we were attending a technical conference in the Austin Convention Center, and I received a bulk text to stop by a vendor's booth and check out their latest gadget. I did. Got a free T-shirt. Quite powerful. Use it, but with common sense.

Collaterals

As mentioned earlier, collaterals are the client interface tools used by the team. These tools have been around since the dawn of time, so there is no need to provide an in-depth analysis. Brochures, catalogs, project sheets, Statement of Qualification documents, presentations, technical data sheets, technical white papers, and business cards are examples of a few. These tools can be either printed or digital or both. Make is easy for the client to get them if they so desire, and make them available and usable for the customer-facing employees.

Create a brand standard for each of these and enforce them. Consistency is the key. If some employees have pink business cards with flowers and some are plain white with Times New Roman block print, the client feels a very real dysfunction that may never be vocalized. Be a good steward of your brand.

Many companies elect to have downloadable brochures and product information PDFs placed on the website so clients and prospects can easily access whatever is important to them. Great idea; just be sure it's monitored and managed well. Items can become outdated quickly, and nothing screams mediocrity more than outdated stuff on your website.

Presentations fall into the collateral category as well. These visual brochures are simply another way to identify pain points and solutions. Putting the presentation on a memory stick is always a great idea because if the client asks for a copy, you can just give them the stick. Preferably one with your logo on it.

Creating and delivering client presentations digitally through software like PowerPoint and Prezi allows sales folks the luxury of sharing one on one or to an entire auditorium.

 The only caution is to never put proprietary or confidential information on a PowerPoint that is disseminated to a sales force, thinking it will not be shared or copied. Anything that is digital can be shared with the world with the touch of a button.

SYSTEMS AND CRM SOFTWARE

The business development trilogy is a three-pronged machine with a strong need to capture, store, manipulate, and share information. This data system can take many forms. Enterprise-wide systems like SAP, Oracle, Microsoft, Deltek, and CDW will have the capability to provide the BD functions required. Smaller companies choose to manage themselves with systems like Quicken or QuickBooks. That is quite acceptable, however these types of systems do not support business development well and will require a much higher level of manual input and maintenance of BD data. The idea is to ensure that business development and client information is given the same priority as finance, billing, and invoicing data. Many smaller firms use QuickBooks Pro to manage the business and keep the sales and marketing information on the back of a cocktail napkin. Integrate and share information.

We have referred to CRM (customer relationship management) many times throughout this text. Allow me to explain more about this valuable tool. CRM software is a relational database that is used for managing client and potential client information. This database includes items such as company name and static data, personnel contact information, sales orders and opportunities, touches/calls/ appointments, and a variety of customer related items. Most CRM systems can interface seamlessly with the company enterprise system, allowing for dynamic informational exchange and updates, or they can operate as a stand-alone system. Like the website, the more spent, the more elaborate the CRM can be.

Regardless, having a database of some sort for business development activity and information is mandatory, and a CRM is the best way for the business development team to share, maintain, and be organized. Many smaller teams use a series of Excel spreadsheets to maintain the business development information. I have even seen people use a written ledger (back in the 80s). There is absolutely nothing wrong with whatever tool that is chosen, as long someone "owns" the accuracy and integrity of the data, and it is maintained regularly and shared properly.

Devices

Communicating; using and updating CRM-type data, calendars, and schedules; appointment setting; conference calling; presentations; order taking; and customer account analytics are some of the activities that digital devices make smoother and much more efficient. Telepresence/conference software, laptops, notebooks, smart phones, tablets, and iPads enable employees to capture, manipulate, and share information effortlessly. Using these tools allows a freedom that business developers should take every advantage of in the marketplace.

 As devices become smaller, faster, and more user friendly, smart B2B companies encourage their business development leadership to evaluate and embrace any new innovations that make sense.

In addition to these devices, there are many other devices and software tools that are available, depending upon how elaborate you desire to be. Some include the following:

- Sales prospecting automation software
- Webinar/Web conference systems
- Website content management systems
- Tracking and dashboard software
- Graphic design/Photo editing software
- Wireless and Bluetooth devices

What a company chooses to engage and how these tools are used varies greatly. Depending upon budget, industry, product/service, or geography, what works for one may not work for others. The primary message is to use the best tools to gain the best advantage for your clients that you can afford.

The litmus test is, are these tools going to enable our team to better serve our clients, or are they just simply cool?

Evaluating and choosing the technology and tools to support the trilogy is very subjective. Needs vs. wants? Impressive or useful? Price vs. ROI?[60] Sanity is the best guide. If I am building and selling birdhouses from my garage, and I complete one a month, most likely I do not need a high-speed pneumatic nail gun and ten thousand dollars' worth of power woodworking equipment.

---

60. ROI refers to return on investment.

PART 3:

CONCLUDING REFLECTIONS AND OBSERVATIONS

"The more we learn and the more we know, the more we know we don't know." (Kenneth Earnest)

According to the U.S. Small Business Administration, 30 percent of all new businesses fail within the first two years, and 50 percent fail within the first five years.[61] The Small Business Administration also states that only 25 percent of those businesses make it beyond fifteen years.[62] Sort of gloomy, huh?

Why? There are a multitude of opinions about these horrendous statistics. There is also no single answer, but one thing is very apparent: many of these highly enthusiastic entrepreneurs did not develop a comprehensive business plan that included proper due diligence of the market they chose and have *failed miserably to initiate an effective trilogy-based business development strategy.*

All the components of business development we have discussed are paramount to the overall philosophy, but if we boil it down, here are the *four main power points* to remember about the trilogy:

 1. Business development is a concept, not a department.

2. Client loyalty is the single purpose.

3. It is a three-legged team sport:

$$BD = M + S + CS$$

4. TRUST is the true currency of business development.

61. "Top 6 Reasons New Businesses Fail," *Investopedia.* Retrieved from https://www.investopedia.com/slide-show/top-6-reasons-new-businesses-fail/.

62. "Do Economic or Industry Factors Affect Business Survival?" *SBA,* 2012. Retrieved from https://www.sba.gov/sites/default/files/Business-Survival.pdf.

From 2006 to 2009 I served as a volunteer advisor for a State Technology Alliance. This quasi-governmental agency provided Angel funding,[63] mentoring, and assistance to start-up companies in that state and has helped launch hundreds of successful companies that are thriving today.

We had an advisory team consisting of accounting experts, production and operations folks, and sales and marketing people. My role was to provide feedback regarding how these new firms would approach "go-to-market" tactics, sales, and business development of their new "whiz-bang" technology.

Invariably, almost every single one had invested an enormous amount of energy, time, thought, and resources into research, development, and state-of-the-art production techniques and equipment, hired expensive engineers or designers, and set up elaborate accounting systems—but they all had given very little thought to creating *customers*. When I asked about their business development plan, the typical response after a blank stare was, "Well . . . we were just going to hire a couple young people right out of college or possibly even find some contract sales reps to just go out and sell. Our idea is so great, it will virtually sell itself." Most of those companies never got off the ground.

In Part 1 we said that business development is really a philosophy of synergy, and we described the three pillars or interdependent synergies:

- Marketing
- Sales
- Customer Service

. . . and why each is critical to the business development engine of any company.

---

63. "An angel investor is usually a high net worth individual who provides financial backing for small startups or entrepreneurs." Akhilesh Ganti, "Angel Investor," *Investopedia*, 2019. Retrieved from www.investopedia.com/terms/a/angelinvestor.asp.

We have shown how without interrelated harmony, your business development team can *never* reach maximum potential.

Regardless of what you manufacture or sell, without this power of three things working together, no business can sustain life. Simplify things, and just remember:

- *Marketing* carries the message of value to the masses,

- *Sales* makes new friends and influences people one at a time, and

- *Customer Service* understands the needs of our client base and provides whatever is required to ensure sustained client loyalty.

In Part 2 we outlined seven steps to evaluate and improve the business development engine. Not an end-all of answers and absolutes but a thought-provoking exercise that should help identify weaknesses, strengths, and shortcomings that will lead to an evaluation of areas of change or improvement that must be addressed. The mission of this entire section was to assist in ensuring your business development team is structured for the optimum.

If there is a critical message from all this word salad I have created, it would be this repeat statement:

 The key element that most companies fail to embrace is to empower all employees to take ownership in the business development vision, not just the sales folks. Share the vision, strategy, and excitement about whatever you provide with everyone at your company, and in turn, they will carry that message to the clients in ways you did not imagine.

215

> **In B2B, people buy from people, they do not buy from companies.**

In 2018 *Forbes Magazine* and The American Customer Satisfaction Index (ACSI) publicly published a list of the top twenty companies for customer service.[64] In order, these were,

1. Chick-fil-A
2. Trader Joe's
3. Aldi
4. Amazon
5. Lexus
6. Costco Wholesale
7. HEB Grocery
8. Toyota
9. Publix
10. Wegmans Food Markets
11. Subaru
12. Google
13. Apple
14. L Brands
15. LG
16. Texas Roadhouse
17. Cracker Barrel
18. Thrivent Financial
19. FedEx
20. Daimler – Mercedes Benz

---

64. Christopher Elliott, "These Companies Have the Best Customer Service," *Forbes.com*, 2018. Retrieved from https://www.forbes.com/sites/christopherelliott/2018/07/11/these-companies-have-the-best-customer-service-heres-why/#2294620ab80a.

Although these companies are primarily retail and consumer oriented, and this text is about B2B, it is still very important to discuss what makes these companies the best of the best. Because what makes them the best is universal. These companies understand what is important. They have business development engines that *purr*. They understand that customer service is the bedrock that any business development team builds on.

 They know that marketing, sales, customer service, and all the supporting functions involved *must* work cohesively, sharing information and leadership vision.

They *must* be a part of the same team, all pulling in the same direction.

Many of these companies are shining examples of the three pillars of business development in unison. They are collaborative, "single view" customer minded, and demand that all three elements of the trilogy work together in harmony every single day.

If your company's business development efforts are already in sync with the trilogy concepts like these companies are, then take time to applaud yourself and your team. You are certainly in the minority.

If you find that you are not in sync with the trilogy concepts, then the next step will be to take some action.

- Change, Innovate, Execute.
- OWN the changes.
- Be consistent and courageous.
- Be intentional.
- Develop a change plan.
- Make the changes.
- Wash, rinse, and repeat.

217

What is the definition of insanity? "Doing the same thing over and over again and expecting different results."

Change is hard. Admitting that we were doing things wrong is even harder. But the first step in any thousand-mile journey is the most important. The easy thing to do is nothing. I asked at the onset if you would simply be open minded. Consider and digest all this information, then apply it to your company or situation in a manner that works best for you and your team. Then make a plan and take some action. You will be amazed at the outcome.

Good luck, and Godspeed!